ONE MAN'S WHITCHURCH

A Step Back in Time

Terry Chard

Text Copyright © Terry Chard 2025
Design Copyright © Alice Hunt 2025
All rights reserved.

Author has asserted his right under the Copyright, Designs and Patents Act 1988 to be identified as the author of this work.

No part of this book may be reprinted or reproduced or utilised in any form or by electronic, mechanical or any other means, now known or hereafter invented, including photocopying or recording, or in any information storage or retrieval system, without the permission in writing from the Publisher and Author.

First published 2025
by Rowanvale Books Ltd
The Gate
Keppoch Street
Roath
Cardiff
CF24 3JW
www.rowanvalebooks.com

A CIP catalogue record for this book is available from the British Library.
Paperback ISBN: 978-1-83584-168-6

To:

        Rhian and Ceri,
     Tobi, Ethan and Seren,
        Tom and Tony.

                One and all, my rock.

Contents

Introduction 15

Treoda 21
    The name.. 27
    The Romans... 29

Melingriffith (The Ancient Mill) 32

Y Wenallt 35

Proper History 37
    Llewelyn Bren.. 42

Medieval Map..44
    Population Change 47

Booker and Velindre 50

The Melingriffith Works 56

A Bus Terminus 61

Whitchurch Common 63

Shows, Competitions and Entertainment.68
    Horticultural shows 71

Local News 75
- Crime and punishment 76
- It's a hard life 81
- The mystery of the miller 85
- It's not such a hard life 87
- Then as now 89

Whitchurch Pigs 91
- Swine fever 95
- Bacon galore 97

Whitchurch Parish Council 98

The Coryton Railway 100
- The train and the tithe barn 102

Buildings of Interest 104
- Ty Mawr 104

Island Cottage 108

The Willows 110

Whitchurch Vicarage 111

Woollen factory 113

The Church 114
- The old parish church (Old Church Road) 114
- St Mary's Church 120
- St Mary's church hall 123

Other Places of Worship ... 125
Ararat Church ... 125
Bethel Church ... 127
The Tabernacle ... 129
Whitchurch Methodist Church (Wesleyan Chapel).129
St Teilo's Roman Catholic Church ... 130

Sport ... 131
Whitchurch Association football ... 131
Whitchurch rugby ... 132
Whitchurch cricket ... 134
Amalgamation of clubs ... 135
Whitchurch hockey ... 135
Athletics ... 137
Bowls ... 139
Prize fighting ... 140
Cycling ... 141
Tennis ... 142
Polo ... 143
Hunting ... 145
Other sports ... 146

Societies ... 150

Places of Note ... 153
Bonzo (Bondo?) Hill ... 153
The Glamorganshire Canal ... 154
An idyllic life? ... 161
Whitchurch Library ... 162

Whitchurch Hospital ... 165
- Negotiations ... 167
- Hold-ups and setbacks ... 171
- The hospital opens, but the problems continue 175
- The tower ... 178

Tragedy ... 179

Public Services ... 182
- The post ... 182
- Gas, electricity and water ... 184
- Sewerage ... 188

Royal Visit ... 190

Pubs ... 191
- The Plough ... 192
- The Fox and Hounds ... 194
- The Hollybush (Llwyncelyn) ... 195
- The Maltsters ... 196
- The Masons Arms ... 197
- The Royal Oak ... 199
- The Three Elms ... 200

The Possible Origin and Meaning of............203

References 205

Attributions...207

Useful Resources..208

Author Profile...212

Before we start...

Do you think you know Whitchurch well? Let's see how you get on with these questions:

- There is something in Whitchurch to commemorate the golden jubilee of Queen Victoria's reign in 1885, and it is still there now. Where and what is it?
- Where was the white church that identified our village?
- Why is Whitchurch accepted in Welsh as being Eglwys Newydd (New Church) rather than Eglwys Wen (White Church)?
- Where was the square?
- Where was the crossroads?
- Where was the lane of the slope of the corpses?
- Who was the notorious Welsh robber Sian Goch?
- Why is there a large circle on three sides of the tower at Whitchurch Hospital?
- Where and what is a batter?
- Where was the polo ground?
- Where was Bonzo Hill?
- Was there really a windmill in Whitchurch?

Don't have the answers? How can you sleep at night!

Fear not, you will find these facts, plus many more fascinating details about the history, culture and customs of Whitchurch, in the chapters that follow.

ONE MAN'S WHITCHURCH

Introduction

As a Whitchurch man, born, bred and schooled here, after seven decades, I thought I knew it pretty well. Then I found in later life that I didn't. I discovered more and more, so much so that I am now motivated to put pen to paper, inspired by my friend and fellow local history 'buff' Nigel Lewis who has done exactly that with his book *101 Things You (Probably) Didn't Know About Whitchurch*.

We sometimes think back with rose-tinted glasses on what life was once like. After having had the privilege of giving some talks to the Reminiscence Group at Whitchurch Library, for AWEN (Arts Whitchurch Eglwys Newydd – the voluntary group based there), I thought it would be worth sharing my discoveries more widely, with a quick mention of gratitude to Nigel and his wife Chris, who do such a great job organising the group, and to all the regulars for their kind support. So, you can now reminisce at home in the comfort of your living room. Grab a cuppa as we open...

A WINDOW INTO THE PAST.

In my early days (1950s vintage), Whitchurch was a village in its own right, on the outskirts of Cardiff. The seemingly endless consumption of green spaces has now rendered it an ordinary suburb of an ever-expanding city boundary. Whitchurch, however, hides an extraordinary backstory, one of ancient conflict, mystery, the weird and the wonderful.

The neighbourhood of Whitchurch once formed part of the old parish of Llandaff. Over the centuries, our village has undergone considerable change, a large part of it within my lifetime, not all of it for the common good. Much of it is detrimental to Whitchurch's history and heritage, a lot of which you would know nothing about unless you set out to look for it, and books of this type can only offer a glance. An attempt to deal adequately with the subject from an historical and antiquarian point of view would require a whole series of weighty tomes, there is so much to share. We will deal with some 'heavy' history; it can't be avoided as it gives us the very basis for our existence here. We'll then pass through time, looking at numerous episodes that shaped the Whitchurch story, some of which would have been witnessed by my most recent ancestors. Whitchurch possesses more than just a passing interest for any type of historian.

However, technology continues to provide a wealth of resources, and there is plenty of online material to keep you occupied for years. This book was never intended to be an in-depth history lesson; it's just a light, casual read that will, I hope, plant a seed of interest.

There are some good books on the history of Whitchurch, most notably *Old Whitchurch: The Sto-*

ry of a Glamorgan Parish by Edgar Chappell (1945) and *Whitchurch – A Brief History* by Hilary Thomas (1982). As you can see, these books were written a good while ago, so it is certainly time for another. I have done my best to bring hard history to the streets I grew up on, rather than simply repeat what is already contained within other books. However, while I add to what is already known, it is inevitable that in part, I will cover the same subjects. The authors that have gone before me are, after all, talking about the same place as I am.

We are blessed in Wales. Many of our towns, villages and farms retain names that have some connection to their past: perhaps a landmark, a particular person or an event. Unfortunately, some of these names have been corrupted, or wrongly interpreted by detailed mapping in the late 18th and early 19th centuries, when surveys and cartography were completed by people with no knowledge or understanding whatsoever of Welsh language and culture.

Almost everywhere you go in Whitchurch, there is an interesting past, whether from an historical industrial process or an old farm. Some of the area, street and road names contain tell-tale signs if you know what to look for, and even our pubs have hidden historic origins.

Whitchurch is very much a case of:

HISTORY ON OUR DOORSTEP

AND

ARCHAEOLOGY WRITTEN IN THE LANDSCAPE.

So, what's the story? Why all the interest?

Well briefly, without the Taff Gorge (Tongwynlais / Taffs Well) and the River Taff, it is unlikely that the village would be here at all. The same applies to Cardiff, for that matter; both exist entirely because of the River Taff, which at the end of the last ice age cut through a natural fault line at the gorge as it flowed to the sea (my old geography teacher told me that).

Along the way, a lot of factors have shaped the village into what we have today. Many Whitchurch residents are not Cardiff people – although I'm a local man born and bred, my birth certificate is stamped Caerphilly Council. Why would that be?

Let's find out what made our village unique, from early human occupation to a Roman settlement; the Anglo-Norman takeover; the church; local industry and, not least of all, the people – ordinary folk that once made this place their home.

One thing to make clear from the outset is just how small Whitchurch once was. To this day, many local people refer to the shopping area simply as 'the village', even though Whitchurch was actually divided into two distinct parts: the Upper Village (Pentre Uchaf) and the Lower Village (Pentre Isaf). The Upper Village, which was the area around the Fox and Hounds pub and the old parish church, was known as Treoda or Treoda Uchaf. The Lower Village was the area in and around the Maltsters. Between the two was nothing but fields and meadow, with a convenient track/footpath running alongside the banks of the brook. The two villages were – and are – just a few minutes apart on foot, with the path diverging to the bridge near the Maltsters in one direction, just as it does today, and the Three Elms, now the route of Mervyn Road, in the other.

It is sometimes difficult to research the history of Whitchurch, partly because of the various names it has been known by over the centuries and a constantly changing parish boundary. Whitchurch or Whitechurch was also known as Album Monasterium; Tre Oda; Kibor; Castellum Kibur; Blank Minster and Blancminster. On top of this, it is also associated with Capel y Stuntaf and Capella de Stuntaf, derived from the term Ystum Taf – bend in the river. Album Monasterium is Latin for White Minster or White Church, and Blancminster means the same in French. Other spellings such as Egluis Newith muddy the water a little. On top of that, the area comes under the ancient identity of Gwaun Treoda (Treoda Heath), which is now the identity of Whitchurch Common, but was once much larger and part of a vast stretch of land, the Great Heath, formerly known as Mynydd Bychan, the lesser heath closer to Cardiff being Y Waun Ddyfal.

At one time, the parish boundary included parts of what we now know as Llandaff North, Tongwynlais, Llanishen, Thornhill, Rhiwbina and Birchgrove. Consequently, some of Whitchurch's local history is inevitably 'borrowed' from other areas, as seen in this example from an advertisement: "The Lease of Rubina [Rhiwbina] Farm situate in the parish of Whitchurch", which was up for sale by auction in February 1809. These communities are all linked; we are a 'family'.

The enjoyment of local history research comes from discovery, finding things that have lain hidden for an age, perhaps decades, centuries or millennia. Concatenation – linking one thing to another – is a rainy-day hobby; luckily, we get a lot of rain in Wales.

If you do find yourself drawn to research the history of Whitchurch, a note of caution: whatever local books or websites you consult, use yourself as a coarse filter. Some things might not be as they seem and we are far away from when it all happened. You can only rely on what has been recorded – somebody else's version or interpretation of events, while you are the 21st-Century forensic judge.

Let us go back to the beginning, to two places that are the focus of interest. One is Treoda and the other is the well-known Melingriffith. We will then take it from there. This bit can get a bit heavy, but do stick with it; after 1800, there's a huge change.

Treoda

Treoda is so ancient – evidence of the Bronze Age has been found there – it's perhaps deserving of its own book. Some recognise it as being the site of Whitchurch Castle, but that is probably one for the local Tourist Board to answer, if the area ever gets one.

Treoda is just behind the Fox and Hounds pub. Older locals will remember the mound there, flattened in 1966 for the construction of the Clos Treoda apartments. When archaeologists Jeremy Knight B.A. and Eric J. Talbot B.A. undertook a survey at that time, they described the phases of construction of the mound, detailing the layers of build material.

An inner mound had existed independently, and much later, an outer mound was built over it. The whole inner mound was bowl-shaped, leading the archaeologists to state that it was "difficult to escape the conclusion that it was a Bronze Age barrow". A ditch surrounded the primary mound and in it they found "four small abraded sherds [sic] of pottery of prehistoric character fully consistent with the mound being a Bronze Age barrow". (Ref *The Excavations of a Castle Mound and Round Barrow at Tre Oda, Whitchurch* by Jeremy Knight B.A. – Inspector of Ancient Monuments

– and Eric J. Talbot – Dept of Archaeology, University of Glasgow.)

Before this date, however, the Treoda site had previously been surveyed by G.T. Clarke, an engineer at the Dowlais Works and a renowned archaeologist, in 1848. Unfortunately, he never published his notes. The 1840 tithe map shows the land on which the Treoda mound stood as being owned by a Mr David Rowland, and Clarke only refers to what he had been told by the owner rather than recording his own findings.

Clarke's notes state: "Mr. Rowland tells me he cut off about 5ft from the top, filled up the ditch and built his house and others with the stones, many of which were ashlar. He knew nothing of the stones till he began to work...At the E. side he found some very well-built and strong walling with what he thought was a trace of a gateway with portcullis groove. He also found two silver coins of, I think Edward I."

The ashlar mentioned here is simply stone cut and shaped to create a particular form. Rowland only assumed the suggestion of a portcullis groove, something not seen by anybody else. There is an implication that at some point, there might have been evidence of a stone keep. However, thoughts are that "The mention of a gateway with portcullis on the E. side would discount any idea of a round keep."

What is certain is that Rowland had lowered the height of the mound by approximately 5 foot. There was no trace of any masonry found in the rescue excavations of 1966.

The mound has been assumed by some to have had a motte, or stone tower, on top of it. This may be so, although there is no evidence of there ever having been a bailey – an enclosed area of land surrounding the motte. However, some reliable sources mention a barton (Ref: *Old Whitchurch* by Edgar Chappell), possibly the home or farm of a lord of a manor. The suggestion that it was a manor and a central place of administration is the reason that the main A470 in this area is named Manor Way.

If in fact a tower / fort / castle was built there, it is likely that it was never finished, as we will find out later. According to Knight and Talbot's report, there is "documentary evidence that the site was neglected and fell into disuse after final rebuilding in 1314–15".

The mound dimensions c.mid-1800s must have been an approximately 40-metre diameter across the base, 3.6 metres of height and a 28-metre diameter across the top. (Ref: the Knight and Talbot report.)

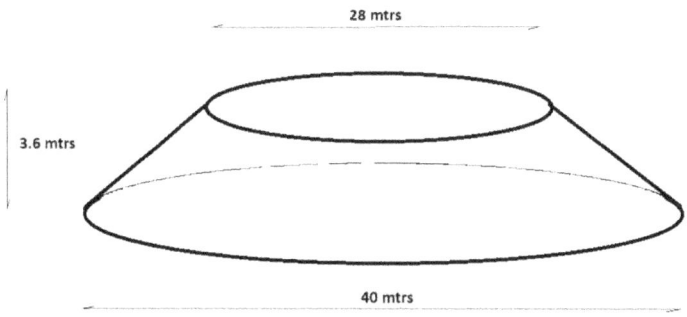

Treoda mound dimensions

There is mention of a "fortelletum newly built at Whitchurch 1317", which confuses things, and of a ruinous castle noted by a man called Leland, a notable antiquarian c.1539 who wrote an account of Glamorganshire at that time. The mottes at both Cardiff Castle and Treoda are described in the Royal Commission on the Ancient and Historical Monuments of Wales (RCAHMW) *Early Castles* as being two of four mottes in the county which were given masonry defences, the other two being at Castell Coch and Swansea.

Another interesting part of Treoda is the mention of a mansion within Mr Rowland's grounds and that his 19th-Century house, destroyed in 1966, stood on the site of a previous house that was regarded as ancient in the 16th Century. With this in mind, the RCAHMW concludes, "The proximity of the castle and church permits no doubt that the former was the administrative centre of the lordship" (ref: Royal Commission of Ancient Monuments, Glam. Inventory, Vol. IV, SECTION MM: MASONRY CASTLES BUILT OVER MOTTES). Clearly, Treoda was a place of strategic importance when it came to local or even perhaps regional governance.

As far as Treoda is concerned, there are many more conflicting and confusing accounts, making it difficult to determine what is factual. It has been described as a 'certain' timber castle (motte), and alternatively as a 'certain' masonry castle. What might be of interest here is that structures started off as timber constructions for speed, before being built in stone later. The location of the mound, however, seems to be the ancestral home of some distinguished local historical figures.

The Archaeologia Cambrensis archive describes it as: "Treoda, now destroyed, was the seat of Yorath Mawr, a descendant of Iestyn. His descendant sold it to David ap Richard Gwyn, whose son Edward was of Llanishen and ancestor in the female line, of the Lewis of that place and of Greenmeadow. Richard Williams, Cromwell's direct ancestor, was of Whitchurch and a cadet of the Lewises of Llanishen, whose arms and quarterings were used by the Protector." (Iestyn – lock that name away for a moment, we will come across him later.)

It was also mentioned in 1570 by Rhys Meurug (aka Rice Merrick, died 1586–7): "This name is applied to a small castle mound or motte lying on Whitchurch brook which forms part of its moat."

There are conflicting dates as to the site being first mentioned: "1295. Gilbert de Clare died seised [sic] of Whitchurch manor." Also: "Treoda Castle Mound marked the site of a medieval castle first mentioned in 1314 and probably built in the later thirteenth century." (Ref: *Old Whitchurch* by Edgar Chappell.) (More on this in a section on Llewelyn Bren.)

The castles around Cardiff are said to shed light on the extent and nature of William the Conqueror's initial settlement and only two of these sites may be identified with recorded medieval manors (Treoda and Castell Coch) "with both only being known in a manorial context from the 13th century". To add to the confusion, we are further told in the *Brut y Tywysogion* A.D. *831*: "The Saxons of Mercia came at night unawares and burnt the Monastery of Senghenydd, which was then where the castle now is and from thence they came to the castle of Treoda which they burnt also. From thence they escaped across the Severn Sea." However, you need to be careful with this particular one; it is believed to be the work (imagination) of Iolo Morganwg (d.1826), someone who is considered by historians to be a little fanciful with his writings, one author adding the caution, "Morganwg was a renowned literary forger."

Whatever is said and done, the Treoda mound was flattened in 1966 for the development that now stands there. It is interesting to note that the mounds at both Morganstown and Rhiwbina (Twmpath – see later in this chapter) are protected: "The monument is of national importance for its potential to enhance our knowledge of medieval defensive practices. The monument is well preserved and an important relic of the medieval landscape. It retains significant archaeological potential, with a strong probability of the presence of both structural evidence and intact associated deposits. (Ref: CADW.) The mound at Treoda clearly did not have the same value and recognition.

From the archaeological surveys undertaken at the mound, we know that the site showed evidence of early occupation (Bronze Age). Iron Age settlements at Caerau (Ely) and at the Wenallt are well known, and Whitchurch lies in between them. It is conveniently located on a flat plain close to a running water supply, a Roman road just a mile away. The earliest site and whatever structure was there likely evolved over time, developing into some kind of fortification, possibly by Roman intervention and later by Anglo-Norman expansion once our native Welsh lords and ancestors were dispossessed of their lands. Eventually, it simply reverted to a peaceful dwelling and a present-day site of historic interest.

The mound has been described as possibly being a shell keep. Recalling the dimensions from the sketch, you can make your own mind up: a keep, a tower? Possibly... but a castle?

Clarke's survey extended beyond the confines of the Treoda site and he did come across some interesting finds in and around the old parish church (opposite the Fox and Hounds). Some of these were Roman. But, before we go there...

The name

One thing that can't be overlooked is the question of the name Treoda. The general understanding is that Treoda comes from the Welsh *Tre* or *Tref,* meaning the home, homestead, or place, of Oda. The survey of Roath and Keynsham in 1702 describes it as "the Dump or bank on the common called Wain Troda". 'Dump' could be an Anglicised misunderstanding of the Welsh 'twmpath'. Twmpath is believed to have originally signified a barren hill or hillock – it is comprised of twyn, a hillock (abbreviated to twm), and paith (shortened to pa'th) for barren. The twmpath in Rhiwbina was commonly called by us locals the 'twmp'.

The name Oda is believed to be Germanic in origin, but the real question is, who was Oda? This question has never been answered, but there are some possibilities.

Odyn or Odin, from the old Norse Audun, was a prominent name in Cardiff in the 13th Century. A John Odyn suffered imprisonment for befriending Llewelyn Bren, who was connected with Whitchurch (we will come across Llewelyn shortly). The Treoda name, though, seems to pre-date this link.

An Oda was Bishop of Ramsbury between 925 and 927. The Archbishop of Canterbury in 942 was said to be the son of a Dane who came to England in 866, but no connection could be found between him and this neck of the woods, and it seems unlikely that anyone of Danish descent would have been welcome here at that time. Whoever Oda was, he / she surely must have been accepted and well established locally to have had their name linked to the site for this length of time.

Unfortunately, the question still remains unanswered. Unless, of course, you want to take up the challenge.

The Romans

The archaeological survey of Treoda in 1966 and the notes of G.T. Clarke's findings both refer to there having been a Roman settlement in the area. The old maps (1875) (Ref: National Library of Scotland) show the outline of what was a "Roman Station supposed remains of". This location is now occupied by the houses and gardens on the north side of Ty'n y Pwll Road with the tennis club just behind, as in the sketch below. Clarke, however, discovered more:

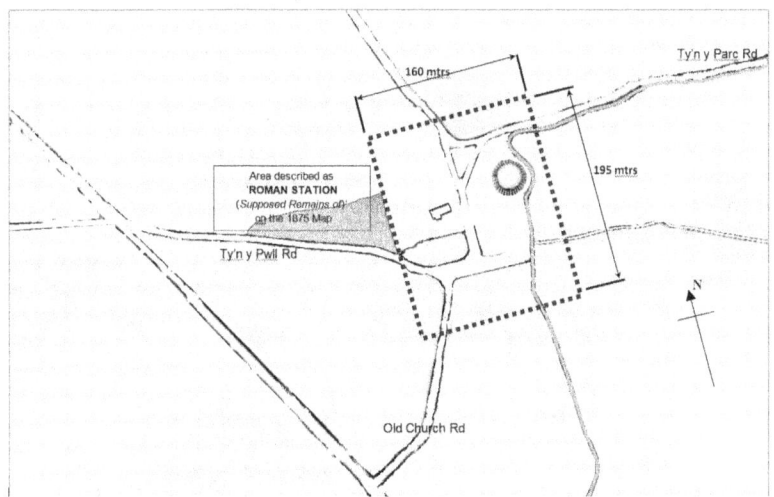

Sketch showing Clarke's outline of a Roman settlement.

The settlement surveyed by Clarke, shown as a dotted rectangle, was described as being approximately 195 metres x 160 metres (dimensions quoted Ref. *Glamorgan – Early Castles*, Royal Commission on the Ancient and Historical Monuments of Wales) and seems to be aligned in a northerly direction. There is little evidence of it now; the centre of it is more or less at the entrance to the Fox and Hounds car park. This settlement enveloped the Treoda mound, Bronze Age in origin. The Romans commonly occupied such sites in order to impose their authority on the land and local inhabitants.

From the sketch, it is not too difficult to imagine the routes / tracks in and out of the settlement; these form the roads we still use today. Heol y Forlan is a modern road, but it is reasonable to assume that there might have been a track running northwards from the enclosure. Of interest is the route along Ty'n y Parc Road, which leads to Caerphilly Road, known to be the Roman road to Gelligaer. The route along Ty'n y Pwll Road leads to Velindre Road and to what became Melingriffith and the river. I wonder whether there would have been a mill there at that time, but that is pure speculation.

One feature of this Roman settlement does still remain at the west edge. This is in the form of a very short length of raised bank on the boundary of Whitchurch Tennis Club at the south-east corner of the courts.

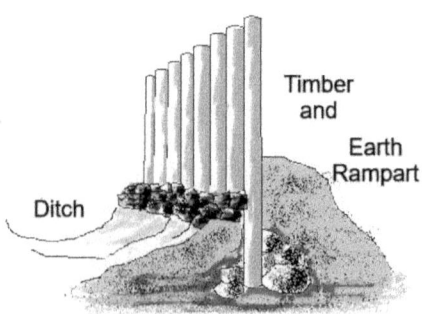

This sketch shows a typical section of a Roman rampart structure, comprising a timber parapet and a ditch on the outside. The rubble from the digging of the ditch was used to build a raised bank on the defended side.

The tennis club is currently under threat. It would be a great shame to lose a facility of this stature, not just for the village, but for the entire region. It would be an even greater shame – irresponsible even – if this last remnant of our ancient history and heritage, as well as any underlying archaeology, is lost forever to careless and inconsiderate development.

I am left to wonder how much of our ancient past is still undiscovered and whether any archaeology remains under our feet.

Melingriffith
(The Ancient Mill)

There is no doubt that Treoda is the most ancient part of Whitchurch, but Melingriffith (Melin / Felin = Mill, so the name means Griffith's Mill) played a significant part in the evolution and development of our village, mostly due its industrial past. For more on who the Griffith in question was, see the 'Proper History' chapter.

A mill was owned by the Welsh lord of this part of the land until the Normans came. It would have been an essential part of the economy, processing grain for local producers and use, and for trade; a desirable asset for the landowner and a lifeline to much of the population, as sparse as it might have been. Positioned on the bank of the River Taff, the mill might have been driven directly by river flow, or perhaps water was diverted along a millstream / leat to power it. There is now a feeder that runs from Radyr weir, but this was a much later construction.

A 14th-Century map of this area shows a mill located at the bend in the river, an area you might well know of. According to research records, the manor of Whitchurch was not created until c.1267 when a clause in the important Agreement of Woodstock 1126 between Earl Robert of Gloucester (Robert pronounced the French way) and Bishop Urban of Llandaf conceded "all claims the bishop had made against the earl's men, in lands they claimed were not held by the bishop". These lands included Whitchurch, but the chapel of Stuntaf (Ystum Taf – the bend in the river) was granted to the bishop, along with other land donated by the earl.

Here's an important extract from another source: "Now lost, the chapel lay near the river about a mile west of Treoda." (*Old Whitchurch* by Edgar Chappell). This places it at the site of the old mill, Melingriffith, and this church / chapel is the original White Church, Album Monasterium or Blancminster. Whichever way it's described, it is only likely to have been a basic, modest place of religious worship and gathering, perhaps originally a mill building with whitewashed stone outer walls.

The old mill would have to have been a robust building with substantial foundations in order for it to withstand the extreme river conditions and last so long. In ruin much later in its life, it became the iron plate rolling mill and tin works more readily identified with the area, and is now the site of a 1970s housing estate.

Forest Farm had been associated with the works for almost two centuries, but it was not included in the will of Lewis Lewis, who owned other farms in the area, in

1735. (It's interesting to note he was not the same Lewis Lewis we read about later in the 'Pubs' section.) There is a suggestion that at this time, the mill was water driven from a watercourse run from Radyr weir.

In the Booker and Blakemore eras (see the 'Booker and Velindre' chapter), the tin works operated in conjunction with the iron works at Pentyrch. Local tradition has it that this started with the Lewis family, quite probably the New House branch. There is evidence to suggest that the Pentyrch works was started in the reign of Henry VIII by Sir William Mathew of Radyr.

Many of the old Melingriffith records were destroyed in the 1930s following closure of the works, but there is evidence of a surviving lease dated 1754, and common wisdom suggests the mill must have been used for industrial purposes, rather than agricultural. Who knows? Maybe the foundations of that ancient mill are still there somewhere.

Y Wenallt

Close to the ancient centres of Whitchurch there is evidence of an Iron Age settlement on y Wenallt. The RCAHMW has it recorded, but Cardiff Council, which now owns it as part of Cardiff Parks, has no mention of the Iron Age settlement on its website. Neither is it on that of the Woodlands Trust, both bodies preferring to focus on the natural habitat. Quite why the settlement remains obscure is curious.

The Iron Age settlement is just 1.6 miles away from the Treoda barrow. The sketch below is taken from a LIDAR image of the area, LIDAR being a laser-scanning process that captures what lies below by ignoring trees and undergrowth to expose the underlying land. Banks and footpaths can clearly be seen.

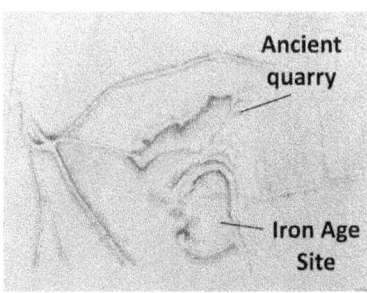

Wenallt Iron Age settlement

Centre top of the sketch is an anomaly, which has been identified as an ancient quarry, below the play and picnic area of past and present-day visitors. South of the quarry is an oval ear-shaped land form, a plateau, and this is the site of the Iron Age settlement. Few will know of this and even fewer have seen or could locate it.

This section on the Wenallt had to be included. It is not part of the Whitchurch of modern times, but has links with our ancient past and the history that exists around us. It cannot be ignored, particularly so because of the lack of information available on it.

Proper History

Let's now put some meat on the bones. Essential history – we can't avoid it. It's ours. So, here comes a quick crash course that will have the purists pulling their hair out.

Iestyn ap (son of) Gwrgant (1014–1093) was a key figure in the fate of our village and South Wales in general, and he is linked to Treoda. Before the Conquest, he was Lord (or Prince) of Glamorgan. This was a time when Wales was divided into regions, each with its own king, and Iestyn's son Rhydderch (Roderick) was self-appointed King of South Wales, but he was killed in a battle over territorial claims on the border of South and West Wales.

At the time, Rhys ap Tewdwr was the overlord of West Wales. Iestyn, out of revenge and in no small measure to preserve the boundaries of the region, needed to remove the threat that Rhys imposed. In a nutshell, a few other native barons, one being Einon ap Collwyn, whom Port Eynon, Gower, is named after, also had some variance with Rhys, and they all joined forces with Iestyn. Despite this alliance, Iestyn still considered Rhys to have the advantage, anticipating him having assistance from the North Wales regions and Ireland (some of Viking descent).

What happened next was a seismic shift in the fortunes of our lands. The Iestyn Alliance enlisted the help of Robert Fitzhamon, the feudal baron of Gloucester, through Einon in order to strengthen their forces. Up until this point, the Normans had stayed out of Wales. Legend has it that Einon had served the King of England William II in France, and so was well connected with the Anglo-Norman barons.

This set the scene for a battle between the two forces, East and West, a confrontation that brought Rhys eastwards. The battle took place near Hirwaun (Herwenorgan) c.1093. Here, Rhys was defeated.

Iestyn had offered various rewards to secure the support of his Welsh allies. In the aftermath of the battle, so the history books tell us, he failed to honour his promises of reward, one of which was the hand of his daughter Nest in marriage to Einon, a promise he denied ever making. Robert Fitzhamon, it seems, acted as arbitrator, but failed.

This led to a showdown, in which Robert Fitzhamon demonstrated some tactical genius. He strategically positioned his fighting force at the edge of the battle site, looking over it from an elevated position. His plan / tactic was to enter the affray when Iestyn's force showed signs of weakening, thereby ensuring victory. Some, however, believe that his true intention was to enter the battle in support of whichever side was gaining the upper hand, making sure to be on the victorious side in a position of strength.

In the face of overwhelming odds, Iestyn was defeated, but he escaped. Legend has it that he became a monk at Keynsham Abbey where he saw out his days, but it wasn't built at that time. More likely, he might have seen out his remaining life in France.

You might be excused for thinking all this is a bit contrived and that history is written by the victors. It seems a clever plan, to set up a rival in a power struggle, claiming he has promised all sorts of riches and rewards in return for loyalty and support, knowing that the promises would never be met and that the supporting allies would eventually feel hard done by. There was only ever going to be one winner.

This battle between Iestyn and his former allies is believed to have taken place at Rhiwbina (hence the Bloody Brook – Nant Waedlyd), although some sources place it at the Small Heath. After this power struggle, out of all the depleted combat forces, it was Robert Fitzhamon who held the cards. His army was the least affected by the battle; the others, it is said, lost half their men, so Fitzhamon now had the balance of power, so much so that he established himself at Cardiff.

He then set about sharing the riches of the land among his favoured fellow barons, as he had apparently promised them. The Normans now had their foot in the door in South Wales, a key moment in our history.

The distribution and award of land has been documented in detail. Fitzhamon acquired some of the richest and most productive areas of South Wales, and demanded fealty from his knights and squires as he shared it out. Of interest to us is that the Lordship of Senghenythe (Senghenydd), within which Whitchurch lies, was given to Cedrych ap Gwaethfod. He had been Einon's neighbour and there is a suggestion that they were related. After battle, Einon did take the hand of Nest and they had a daughter Gwenllian. Cedrych's son (Cadifor ab Cedrych) later married Gwenllian.

Are you still with it? Take a moment to catch up, there's more to come.

The original Senghenydd region (cantref) was vast. It stretched from Brecon down to the coast (present-day Cardiff), bounded on the east by the Rhymney River and on the west by the River Taff. With Fitzhamon in control at Cardiff, the boundary of Senghenydd became a stream near what we now know as Maindy. Over the generations and with the passing of time, boundary creep redefined the region, bringing the boundary closer and closer towards Whitchurch, thereby diminishing the Senghenydd cantref.

Ifor Bach, born c.1105, was the grandson of Cadifor ab Cedrych. He inherited and became Lord of Senghenydd – Arglwydd Senghenydd. Due to the encroachment on lands owned by Ifor Bach, folklore has it that in 1158, he and his men scaled the walls of Cardiff Castle at night, stealthily slipped into the earl's living quarters (the Earl of Gloucester, William Fitz Robert) and kidnapped him, his wife and his only child, a young son, and removed them to Ifor's country manor in the hills of Senghenydd. There Ifor held them until the earl officially restored everything he had taken, plus a bit more.

Some suggest that Ifor must have had inside help in order to carry out the stunt. In another twist, it is believed that the earl's daughter, born after the kidnap, later married Ifor's son, Gruffydd. She was just 14 years old at the time.

One thing to note here is that most privileged people, the gentry or uchelwyr, despite all their in-fighting tended to rub shoulders with each other, so there were many dynastic marriages, with men acquiring land and wealth in the process. Not much chance for those who were not so high born.

Gruffydd had a son, Rhys, and in time, Rhys had a son he named Gruffydd, so we have Rhys ap Gruffydd and Gruffydd ap Rhys. It was this Gruffydd that some local landmarks were named after, such as Griffithsmoor east of Cardiff and our own mill in Whitchurch – Melingruffydd (Melingriffith). Rhys ap Gruffydd inherited Senghenydd in 1211, but by then the Welsh hold on the region was under threat from expanding Norman interests.

Llewelyn ap Gruffydd was descended from this line. Some refer to him as Llewelyn of the Wood (Llewelyn Bren), while others interpret Bren as an abbreviation of Brenin – king.

Llewelyn Bren

By Llewelyn's time, encroachment on the lands and properties of Senghenydd had increased, but vast areas still remained in his ownership. One part in 1315 was noted as being a "half built castle in Whitchurch, the uncompleted work of the recently deceased Gilbert de Clare" (Ref. *Llewelyn Bren* by Craig Owen Jones). De Clare is believed to be the builder of Caerphilly Castle.

However, feeling a sense of injustice, and backed by loyal Welsh followers, Llewelyn instigated a rebellion (c.1316, during the reign of Edward II). This led to the destruction of many of the Norman Lords' assets, including the corn and water mills in the district, one of which was at Whitchurch (Melingriffith). However, he spared the manor house at Treoda, this still being in his ownership. All this was in an effort to destroy the regional Norman economy, and the revolt spread throughout South Wales.

It ended when Llewelyn Bren eventually gave himself up, provided that his followers would be spared. He was imprisoned at Brecon along with his two sons. Requests were made to King Edward for Llewelyn to be spared and he was eventually pardoned.

In 1318, Hugh Despenser, the new Lord of Glamorgan, persuaded the king to release Llewelyn into his custody.

Llewelyn was imprisoned at Cardiff Castle where he was tried and condemned as a traitor. Later, he was dragged through the streets, hanged, drawn and quartered, his intestines burnt and scattered. Despenser eventually met the same fate, similarly executed for his transgressions. He's a man loathed for this deed even today.

Llewelyn Bren was buried at Greyfriars, Cardiff. During Owain Glyndwr's raid and destruction of Cardiff in 1404, Greyfriars was spared, in part out of respect for the graves of Llewelyn Bren and John Odyn (mentioned earlier) buried there.

There is plenty of material available on this phase of our history should you ever wish to research at your own leisure.

Medieval Map

One of the earliest maps, if not the earliest that covers our area, is the late Professor William Rees's 1932 interpretation of 'South Wales and the Border – In the Fourteenth Century', held by the British Library and showing features of the land at that time. William Rees was Professor of History at the University of Wales, Cardiff.

As sparsely populated as our current village was back then, there are some significant features worth describing.

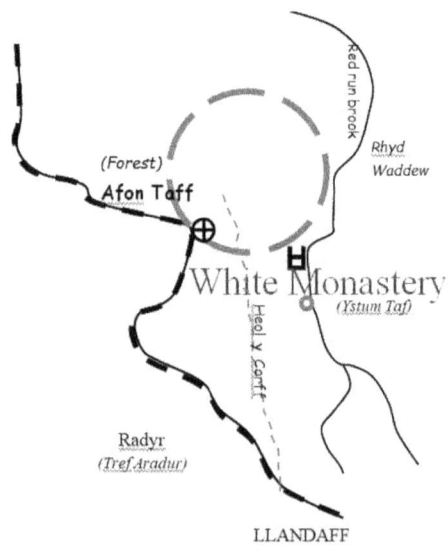

South Wales and the Border – In the 14th Century

The River Taff (Afon Taff) is shown on the left, with an area marked as 'forest' adjacent to the bend in the river known as Ystum Taf, mentioned earlier. On the bend is a spot shown on the map as a circle with a cross. This is the Watermill of the Lord – the Lord in this case being the regional Anglo-Norman Baron. While most of the region at this time was Welsh territory / domain, the area around the mill (shown as a larger circle) was identified as being "Demesnes of Chief Lord" and undoubtedly English. The mill, of course, is the ancient Melin Gruffydd (Melingriffith).

Another feature here is the red run brook, which we know as Whitchurch Brook or Nant Waedlyd, the Bloody Brook. Local legend has it that it was so named after Iestyn's battle near Beulah, Rhiwbina, in which the slaughter caused the water to run red with blood. That is a lot of claret to run into the water, unless, of course, all the poor, unfortunate victims chose to occupy the banks of the stream while they were being slashed to bits in their thousands. It is more likely a result of the watercourse running through natural clay or iron deposits further upstream.

Rhyd Waedlyd (the bloody ford) is / was the crossing at Beulah. On this map, it is written as Rhyd Waddew, although it is difficult to interpret this, being as it's obscure on the original map. The area defined as White Monastery is in close proximity to Ystum Taf. Close by, just on a bend of the red run brook, is the symbol of a lesser castle (English), shown as:

This is the location of the old Treoda mound.

The Common is shown and Gabalfa has an alternative spelling on the original map, but what about Heol y Corff? Hwyl Rhiwr Cyrff is mentioned in Edgar Chappell's book and this route is now known as College Road.

The Chancery Proceedings of 1605 state: "...situate in the said parish of Whitchurch ... and the common way leading from Landaff bridge to Treoda, on the north. And the messuage and 2 closes containing 16 acres of lands lying next the lane called Hewle Rywr Kirff on the west..."

Hewle Rywr Kirff – Heol Rhiw'r Cyrph, or the Lane of the Slope of Corpses, the slope being the change in level as the track descended from Whitchurch to the river. This was in keeping with the agreements made at Woodstock in 1126, mentioned earlier:

"The chapel of Stuntaf and the tithe of that township (vill) and the land which the earl gives to the said chapel in order that a priest may by means of the tithe be maintained. Provided that the parishioners on Christmas Day, Easter and Pentecost visit the Mother Church at Llandaff and the bodies of those who die in the said village be taken to the mother church for burial."

Heol Rhiw'r Cyrph, a corpse road, was the route from the parish to the mother church at Llandaff, the last trip for the deceased as they took their place in the hallowed turf. Dwell on that for a moment. Llandaff Bridge did not exist until much later and the only way to cross the river was by a ford near the weir, or by a boat crossing near Western Avenue bridge.

There was a cost in this. The seasons, the weather – snow, ice, rain, wind or shine – and river conditions would all have had a big part to play. The deceased rarely get to choose their last day on Earth.

Population Change

Browne Willis (1682–1760) was an antiquary, author and politician. He wrote this about Whitchurch:

"...having in it 32 farmhouses and about 25 cottages, and lying at a great distance from the church, procured in Bishop Field's time (1619 to 1627), about the beginning of the reign of Charles 1, a separate chapel to be erected therein for the use of the inhabitants, and is now considered distinct from Llandaff."

This church is a reference to St Mary's, once on Old Church Road (more on this later). At this time, the countryside was entirely agricultural. Browne Willis's piece gives us some idea of the size of Whitchurch all those years ago.

The estimated population in 2011 showed there were 16,138 of us. In 1801, there were just 696:

Year	Population	Year	Population
1801	696	1881	2,752
1811	997	1911	9,079
1821	972	1921	11,287
1831	1,184	1931	12,733
1841	1,376	1951	19,820
1851	1,661	1961	27,325

Although clouded by various parish council boundary changes to electoral wards, these numbers provide a snapshot of the population change over time. The next diagram shows that the population stayed fairly level until 1851, and then started a gradual climb. From 1891 onwards, there was a rapid increase:

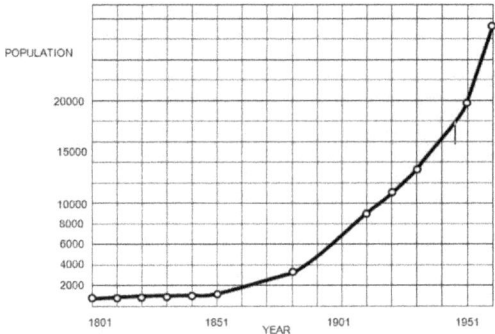

Oddly enough, World Wars 1 and 2 do not seem to have affected the trend.

You could probably draw an identical graph for the development of the English language in the area at the expense of native Welsh. Certainly at the beginning of the 19th Century, almost everybody in the parish spoke Welsh.

The reality is that in the olden days, the entire area was sparsely populated. In the times of early medieval conflict, there was next to nobody here and the land would have been defended by the native Welsh population from a wider area, becoming a no man's land or buffer zone between opposing sides. Even at the beginning of the 19th Century, the number of people here could easily have fitted into a large hall. It would have been very much a case of everyone knowing everyone else.

But then, Whitchurch is a bit like that even now. It is our village.

Booker and Velindre

Most local people will know of the old Melingriffith tin works and the Booker family that owned it for generations.

Thomas William Booker was a highly successful and wealthy businessman who lived in Velindre House – Velindre (Felin / Melin-dre) meaning Place of the Mill – until he died in November 1858. The news of his death resonated throughout the land, the newspapers dedicating columns in homage to him, each one bordered with a ribbon of black to mourn his loss.

His funeral cortege captured the hearts of many. Respectable and well-dressed people crowded the windows of the houses and thronged the streets on foot, on horseback or in carriages, escorting his coffin as it made its way to its final resting place, fresh numbers arriving with every step until the procession was over a mile long. At Whitchurch Common, the cortege was met by workers from Pentyrch and Melingriffith. The papers described it as "one of the most striking and impressive [corteges] we have ever witnessed", and said, "It is computed that at least 8,000 persons were present at this time."

A book could be written about the Booker family alone; suffice to say that T.W. Booker was highly regarded. The son of a clergyman, at an early age, he was adopted by his uncle Richard Blakemore Esq (MP for Wells), whose surname he assumed, becoming Thomas William Booker Blakemore. He had two sons: Thomas William the younger and John Partridge.

When eventually the Booker estate was advertised for sale in July 1881, it was extensive. The family wealth was clear for all to see. It was advertised as follows:

"Highly-Important Sale of Valuable Freehold and Leasehold Estates, Collieries, Mines, and Minerals, including The Melin Griffith Works, and The Pentyrch Works, situate and lying, as regards the Melin Griffith Works, about 3 miles, and as regards the Pentyrch Works, about 5 miles from the important and rising Town of Cardiff, with convenient sidings to the main line of the Taff Vale Railway, and with the Glamorganshire Canal running through the Melingriffith works, containing about 865 acres, 611 acres being freehold, and 254 acres being leasehold. These Properties comprise an area of 513 acres, or thereabouts. There are 69 Cottages on the Freehold Property, comprised in this Lot, together with a residence known as Ynis House.

"The Melin Griffith Works, with 31 acres of Woodland, are held for the remainder of a term of 200 years from Lady-day 1772, at a yearly rent of £205. The works included six tin-plate mills, four driven by steam power and two by water power, and a large tin house with all appliances also five sheet iron mills, two driven by steam power and three by water power, and also a large ochre works. There are 13 Cottages on this property.

"The Pentyrch Works and Lands are held for the remainder of a term of 73 years, from Michaelmas 1867, at rents of £200 and £21 6s. At these works there is a colliery equal to 400 tons a day, 82 coking ovens an iron ore mine, and three blast furnaces; brick works with charcoal and coke bar iron forges with all appliances. There are 50 Cottages on this property.

"Also, the valuable mines and minerals under the freehold lands, and the leasehold mines and minerals of the lands in the Parish of Pentyrch, containing about 2,500 acres, or thereabouts and the mines and Minerals under Garth Hill, about 266 acres, and the freehold mines and minerals under a portion of the Llan Farm, also the fixed plant and machinery and loose plant and stock."

The sale included:

"A farmhouse, farm buildings, and pasture and arable lands and woodland, being portions of the Llan farm and Geddrys, containing 179 acres or thereabouts, situate in the parish of Llantwit Vardre. A farmhouse, farm buildings, three cottages, stable and gardens, pasture and arable land, with a siding to the Taff Vale Railway, the whole containing 53 acres or thereabouts, known as Geddrys, situate in Llantwit Vardre. A comfortable Farmhouse, with convenient farm buildings and pasture and arable known as Ty Newydd, or Newhouse Farm, containing 107 acres or thereabouts, situate in the aforesaid parish of Llantwit Vardre; A piece of productive market garden ground, known as Cae Pwll, in the parish of Radyr, and containing 3 acres or thereabouts. Two Leasehold Pieces of ground, in the parish of Whitchurch, with the messuage, or dwelling-house thereon, known as Heoldon. The leasehold mines and minerals under a farm called Llyn y Brain Fawr, containing 85 acres or thereabouts, situate in the said parish of Pentyrch, held for a term of 42 years from March, 1873. The leasehold mines and minerals under a farm containing 146 acres or thereabouts, situate in the parishes of Radyr and Pentyrch, held for a term of 60 years from September, 1844. The Leasehold Parcels of LAND, being part of Tyn y Berllan and Skibbor Fawr farms, or one of them, situate in the said parish of Radyr and containing 8 acres or thereabouts, held for a term of 99 years from February 1844. The leasehold piece of land, being part of a field called Cae Pwll, in Radyr, containing 77 perches and 46 feet or thereabouts, together with the six messuages erected thereon, known as Teaman's Row, held for a term of 99 years from August, 1847."

Quite an empire. Apart from the wealth, it was a stark reminder of just how heavily industrialised the areas of Whitchurch, Ton, Taffs Well and Pentyrch actually were, and how harsh life must have been for our ancestors who worked in them.

The grave of T.W. Booker Blakemore lies in the old parish church opposite the Fox and Hounds, and his monumental tomb is still there. Whitchurch stonemason Eli Evans designed and created it, receiving praise as having "exhibited considerable artistic skill ... and professional taste of no ordinary kind". Evans lived in Vine Cottage (no longer there) which was near the Three Elms.

The younger T.W. Booker died at his residence Sea Lawn, near Southerndown, in April 1887, at 55 years of age. He was said to have been "much esteemed by all classes" (like his father) and was "of a very genial temperament".

To lighten things up a bit, in October 1898, a local man spoke of an incident at Velindre in the time of the old Mr T.W. Booker.

"Mr Booker had a servant named William Richards who was known as Billy and T.W. had long suspected that Billy had helped himself when sent to the cellar for table supplies. One evening with a party of friends, Mr. Booker decided to put the matter to the test and have a little fun. He called Billy to the dining room, told him to get some wine from the cellar, and added, as a caution, 'Now Billy, mind you don't get drinking in the cellar'. Acting surprised Billy assured his master that he was not in the habit of drinking anything in the cellar. Booker then replied by saying 'I'll test you, get me a piece of chalk' and he pretended to rub chalk on Billy's lips 'Now. [sic]' said Mr. Booker, 'if you drink when in the cellar we shall be able to see when you come back.' Billy secured another piece of chalk on the way to the cellar, and after taking a copious draught of wine and smiling at his smartness, he rubbed the chalk on his lips and armed with the wine bottles, retraced his steps in triumph to the dining room. He was amazed to find himself received with shrieks of laughter."

The Melingriffith Works

The Melingriffith has deep historic value to our village; it really only comes second to Treoda. Many of our ancestors worked there and some didn't come out alive.

In this chapter, we will look at a few accounts to give a little flavour of the industry that put Whitchurch on the map. An interesting report was published on behalf of the Children's Employment Commission in 1842 by Robert Hugh Franks, Esq: 'The Employment of Children and Young Persons in the Collieries and the Iron Works of South Wales, the district of Merthyr Tydvil, the collieries of Monmouthshire, Glamorganshire and Pembrokeshire and on the State, Condition and Treatment of such Children and Young Persons' (see the 'Attributions' section at the end of the book). A section of this report included the Melingriffith Works:

"Melingriffith Tin Works. Parish of Llandaff, Glamorganshire. Messrs. Blakemore and Co."

The report highlighted some of the child workers:

Persons employed:

Males		Females	
Adults	65	Adults	20
Under 18 years	10	Under 18 years	5
Under 13 years	30	Under 13 years	10

"Samuel Humphrey, aged 18, annealer. He has been eight years at the work. He attends the furnace to anneal the sheet metal and works hours daily [sic]. He has three rests in two hours, that is, 18 rests in a day, as after each charge is in the furnace, he has to wait till it gets to a proper heat. [Reads and writes. Attends the Wesleyan's very regularly and has a good scriptural knowledge. He earns from 12s. to 14s. per week.]

"Thomas Smith, aged 12, grease-boy. He has been three years at the work. He was a lusterer [dipper of plates in metal]. He lost the tips of his fingers of his right and [hand] which occurred by his passing the plates too quickly through the shears. He was five years at Mr. Phillip's day school. [Reads and writes well. Knows Scripture well.]

"Francis Roberts, aged 10, plate-opener. She stated she had been at work only two weeks and was never at any other labour before and that her mother had always kept her close to home to nurse the children and the only school she had ever been was the Methodist Sunday School. [She had just gained a knowledge of the letters and was very ignorant and evidently much neglected by her parents. Very indifferent scriptural knowledge.]

"Hannah Rowland, aged 18, scourer. 'I was four years engaged as a rubber which disagreed with me. Scouring the metal is not so unpleasant. I get 7s. 8d. a week and work about nine hours a day. I think I have been between six and seven years at work. I was at Mr. Thomas's day school before where I was taught to read and write. I can shape and make dresses and I was two years at the dress making but the occupation was too confining. I never was instructed in the Catechism but have [sic] fair knowledge of the Scripture.' [Reads very well but can scarcely make a letter.]

"Ann Maddick, aged 15, rubber. She has been at the work for five years and works between 9 and 10 hours a day, sometimes longer and gets on average, 7s. 8d. per week. She rests after every share of rubbing [a share is 75 sheets.]

"'The work is not the most wholesome but it is [sic] never particularly disagreed with me. We get meat almost every day and plenty of it. I have not been to any day school for six years.' [Can scarcely read, very dull at Scripture but counts very well.]

"Thomas Davis, aged 12, cold-roller. He has been six months at cold rolling and was never at any work before. He reads, writes and ciphers very well. He was six years at Whitchurch school. [Has a good knowledge of geography and is extremely well informed in Scripture history.]

"Anthony Rowland, aged 9, pickle and scale boy. He was nine months on the tin plates and now assists in dipping the plates into acid which we call pickling. He works about 12 hours a day and earns 4s. a week. He gets meat every day. He could not read at all. He goes to the Sunday School to learn letters. [He was eating his dinner of good roast meat and potatoes during this examination.]"

In September 1853, "50 principal individuals of the works were regaled by J.P. Booker Esq., in accordance with the wishes of his excellent father T.W. Booker Esq., M.P., at the Maltsters Arms, Whitchurch, to celebrate the starting, by steam power, of three additional rolling mills, in that ancient, extensive manufactory of tin and sheet iron."

As tough as life might have been for people labouring at the works, there were other things to contend with, not least of all the weather. In September 1877, "there was heavy rain and floods to the extent that bridges were swept away, houses and factories submerged and property and livestock destroyed. At Whitchurch the heavy and incessant rains of caused the river Taff to rise to a height which had never before been remembered for many years. The damage was extremely great. Large quantities of corn, baulks of wood, trees, etc., are seen floating down. One field of wheat in the neighbourhood of Melingriffith was nearly all washed away, and a great amount of damage was done to farms adjacent to the river. Melingriffith Tin Works had completely stopped. The water was over the flues of the boilers. A great number of men were put out of work."

When you consider that in those days there was no welfare state, a prolonged period without work would mean severe poverty and possibly even homelessness and starvation for many. So hard though the labour at the works must have been, and however shocking we may find the idea of taking children out of school and putting them to work instead, there was always an alternative that was even worse, and that was to not work at all.

A Bus Terminus

Who could have predicted the controversy that would be caused by the local bus service when Whitchurch was the end of the line on the Cardiff route? In October 1894, the Cardiff Cabs Committee considered an application "made on the parts of the inhabitants of Whitchurch that the North Road buses should be run as far as The Plough Inn, Whitchurch". After deferring the decision, the committee eventually passed the application, only to face problems a few years later.

The service was sometimes referred to as the Brake Service, a brake being a common term for the old carriages (vehicles) at that time (it's a term readers of a certain age might recognise from the 50s for a shooting brake, ie a car with an estate-type body, and is occasionally spelt 'break' just to confuse things). The problem was to find the most suitable location for stationing the brakes and other vehicles. The traditional stand was near The Plough Hotel on Church Road, but an alternative was under consideration adjacent to the Fox and Hounds, and this caused uproar, not least among the owners and drivers of the vehicles, because of the congestion anticipated due to the narrow streets.

In September 1898, a meeting at the Whitchurch Board School (Ty'n y Pwll Road) discredited the Fox and Hounds proposal, and the meeting ended with the resolution to approach the district council to "pitch a length of road sufficient for standing purposes and if practicable also put up a shelter". At one point in the meeting, all the haggling became so animated, the "chairman threatened to call in the police, but peace and good humour prevailed and the closing scene was attended by the singing of the National Anthem".

The service was still causing problems in 1909, when a local man wrote to the newspapers, complaining about the buses being uncomfortable – "There are no water proof coverings for the seats on top in wet weather" – not punctual, and frequently breaking down. He further complained of the road being too narrow and spoilt by the buses, and that the last bus was 11.05 (presumably pm), forcing people to return "at a needlessly early hour".

He must have liked going clubbing!

In December 1910, the Cardiff Tramways Company (Limited) wrote to the Llandaff District Council: "...everything possible was [is] being done to give Whitchurch a good and efficient omnibus service". However, the company pointed out that the roads were in a "shocking condition", and "any stoppages occurring were due to the bad roads". The Council Clerk Mr M. Warren replied that the breakdowns were due not to the bad state of the roads, but to the bad condition of the buses.

Bad buses, bad roads, and that was 1910.

Whitchurch Common

What is now just an open but almost sterile patch of green land is actually a precious part of our history and heritage, and a significant piece of our identity.

The area has been the target of envy from other communities for ages. In 1666–1687, a list of fees, imposed within the Manor and Borough (of Cardiff), bought this reaction:

"Jurors were envious of the rights, liberties and prejudices for ever free common of Pasture, furze, and turf upon the commons near the said Town, called the Great Heath, and little [Heath, by] the grants and charters aforesaid, being yearly unto two years last [past] presented by the Grand Juries of the said Town accordingly, and [that the] adjacent parishes of Roath, Llanishen, Whitchurch, and other places do daily intrude on the said liberty and common of pasture for many years, to the great wrong and detriment of the said Corporation."

Following the Enclosure Acts of the late 18th and early 19th Centuries, various wealthy landowners purchased the lands of the Great Heath, including Whitchurch Common (Gwauntreoda). From the mid-19th Century, for many years, it hosted all sorts of exhibitions, shows and competitions. It was in September 1848 that one of these shows captured the attention of a local reporter, and his observations led to a well-known landmark which to this day stands in the centre of our community.

"We noticed on the ground adjoining the marquee a very handsome plough made on an improved principle by a blacksmith at Whitchurch. It drew considerable attention and was much admired by those who have to do with the cultivation of the soil."

This plough was fashioned by Reuben Lewis, a blacksmith, who set up a beer house at his workshop on the corner of Merthyr Road and Old Church Road. Shortly afterwards, it became known as the Plough Inn. More about Reuben later in the chapter named 'Pubs'.

The following year, in June 1849, the Wauntreoda Floral and Horticultural Show was held, moving the local reporter to pass comment on various aspects of the summer show:

"We noticed some fine specimens of rhubarb by Messrs. Geo. Lewis, Three Elms and Wm. Lewis, Hollybush; a splendid basket of cut flowers by Mr. W. D. Haddock; a prettily devised plough..." Just for the record, the weather was unfavourable, "owing to which the attendance was not so large and respectable".

Over the brook near the Maltsters was an old stone-arched bridge, a village landmark once known as Gwauntreoda Bridge. In April 1858, it was a cause for concern.

"The bridge appears as strong as ever, although it has carried frequently during the last 50 years portions of machinery for the mills, weighing from 12 to 18 tons; its arches are ample which of late have been left so devoid of coating, as to be distinctly traced nearly from one parapet to the other and its width upwards of 14 feet clear of side walls." Some of the coping-stones had been "wantonly thrown" into the brook. The mill mentioned is, of course, Melingriffith.

A columnist for *The Weekly Mail* provided one surprising and remarkable story relating to Whitchurch Common in August 1879 – surprising and remarkable because executions didn't happen too often around here. In an account reporting on various old folklores and tales of the region, he wrote:

"...it was near Melingriffith that the present Lord Chief Justice James first saw the light and received his first lesson in the English tongue and before we leave this narrative in this locality dwelt the notorious Welsh robber, 'Sian Goch' who was executed for her many crimes on a field near Gwauntreoda."

In November 1886, the parish council held a meeting to consider the advisability of making a footpath from the Lower Village (near the Maltsters) across the common to the Philog. Some were against the proposal. A majority, however, were in favour.

At the same meeting, the question of the tollgate came up: "The feeling of the meeting, with regard to the matter, was that steps should be taken to abolish it." A deputation was appointed to find out what measures could "do away with the nuisance".

In February 1899, the issue of common rights came up, with people asking who actually owned Gwauntreoda. The challenge was to consider the rights of the parishioners while taking into account support for the manorial lord, the Marquess of Bute. The Common had been used for profit from the levy of a toll for shows and roundabouts, and this did not go down well with the people. Securing and identifying the boundaries, and "gipsies" were all a cause for concern.

It transpired that some parishioners still held commoners' rights. In various meetings, things warmed up, with "wild gesticulations and pantomimic affairs. Proceedings went no further and the question was allowed to drop." However, in May 1899, the parish council was determined not to let the question remain, submitting a proposal to Lord Bute to resolve all these issues.

In March 1901, the members of the old Whitchurch Parish Council "vacated their seats", satisfied that they had accomplished their term of office. "It was regretted that, in consequence of the death of the late Marquess of Bute a completion could not be carried out in the matter of Whitchurch Common, but it has been agreed that the piece of land shall become the property of the parish and arrangements will be made when the present Marquess attains his majority."

In July 1907, an old well about 25 foot deep and 10 foot in diameter was discovered in the road waste (I'll leave you to imagine what that was) near the Philog. It was covered in timber and about a foot of soil which had partly given way, leading to its discovery.

The well has since been filled in, but just be careful where you walk...

Shows, Competitions and Entertainment

Some things we will never see again, and this chapter describes one of them.

On 28 December 1867, the Whitchurch and Llanishen Ploughing Match was advertised for 1 January 1868 "in two fields adjoining Gwauntreoda Common, belonging to Mr. Harry Wride, Village Farm and Mr. Wm. Clode, Ty'n y Parc, Whitchurch", family names that remain in our village today. The locals clearly expected a mild winter that year.

The competition was for a senior (over 20s) and junior class, starting at 9am to finish ploughing half an acre by 2pm. The prizes for seniors were 1st: £3; 2nd £2; 3rd £1; 4th 10s. For the under 20s it was 1st prize: £2; 2nd £1 and 3rd 10s

(50p now). The competition was open, but "Each competitor must have resided six months in the district, or have followed a team of horses within the above parishes for three months before the day of ploughing. A public dinner will take place at the Three Elms Inn, at 5 p.m. Tickets 2s 6d each". The secretary was the stonemason Eli Evans, of "Vine Cottage, Waentreoda [sic]".

In October 1868, the Whitchurch and Llanishen Ploughing Match was advertised for Tuesday the 20th "in a most eligible field belonging to Mr. John Evans, situate opposite the Village of Whitchurch distant 3 miles from Cardiff". It was open to "all Ploughmen who have been in the service of a Farmer, or have followed a Team of Horses within the Union of Cardiff for the three months preceding the days of Ploughing". You might think that level of detail was a bit of overkill and entirely unnecessary, but these events were fiercely competitive within the farming community, and the main reason for stringent qualification rules was to prevent farmers from bringing in 'ringers': expert ploughmen from other parts of the country. This used to happen, the outfall leading to a lot of incrimination.

A fee of 2s 6d (12½p these days) was payable, returnable to all who competed. To round the day off: "Dinner at the Three Elms, Gwauntreoda at Six p.m. Tickets 2s 6d each". The secretary was again "Eli Evans, Vine Cottage, Whitchurch near Cardiff". Interesting to note 'near Cardiff' as part of an address, for Whitchurch was still being used for postage through the 1950s and 60s.

In October 1869, the Whitchurch Ploughing Match really captured the interest of the farming community, this time from further afield. An all-comers prize of 5 guineas was on offer (£5.25 for those born after 1970). Among the many competitors was the champion ploughman of all England James Barker, in the employment of Messrs Ransome, Sims and Head of the Orwell Works, Ipswich. Barker arrived with a big reputation and a bit of a fanfare. On the day, however, the first prize went to a farm servant from Duffryn.

Perhaps the old adage of pride coming before a fall was at play that day.

Ploughing matches weren't the only sporting events enjoyed by the people of Whitchurch. On the 22 July 1904, the *Evening Express* published an article on the Whitchurch Boys' Walk:

"A walking match, for boys under fourteen, will take place tomorrow afternoon from the Three Cups, Llandaff Yard, to the top of the second hill above the Holly Bush Hotel, Whitchurch, the route being through Whitchurch and back by way of Llandaff Yard. Nearly 40 entries have been received. The first prize is a silver cup and among the other prizes is a suit of clothes. Mr. George Stone, the secretary, is assisted by a strong committee."

The 'top of the second hill' was, of course, Pendwyallt by definition. And what an incentive the named 'other' prize was!

Some sporting exploits were somewhat more memorable. In September 1906, William (Billy) Brian, a trick cyclist, was challenged to ride a bicycle backwards from the Royal George Hotel (corner of Albany Road and City Road) to the Fox and Hounds, Whitchurch. He had to complete this distance of approximately 3½ miles without dismounting and within 30 mins.

Did he do it? What do you think?

Yes, he did, in 13 minutes 21 seconds. Let's hope there was a whole rack of suits waiting for him!

Horticultural shows

One of the earliest shows, if not the earliest, of this kind in Whitchurch was the Melin Griffith Floral and Horticultural Show. In June 1845, it was held at "Wain – Troda [sic] (Whitchurch Common) near Whitchurch".

Here we get to find out who the main movers and shakers were. "This society is under the patronage of T. W. Booker, Esq., of Velindra a gentleman at all times most ready to support and patronise industry." A feature of this event was that the square in front of the Three Elms Inn, especially enclosed for the occasion, was the venue for the show. A "spacious marquee exhibited the vegetables, chiefly grown by the cottagers in the employ of Mr. Booker and their abundance and luxuriance certainly created astonishment even amongst some of the clever horticulturists of Cardiff." There was a section for Amateurs and Cottagers, one for Gentlemen's Gardeners, Amateurs and Cottagers and another for Market and Gentlemen's Gardeners. Many of us modern-day Whitchurch folk would not have qualified.

In 1846, the event was held in June at Gwauntreoda Common under the name of the Whitchurch Floral and Horticultural Society. Morgan and Thomas, sail makers of Cardiff, provided the marquee.

If you wanted to rub shoulders with the great and the good of that day, this was the place to be. "The society's spacious tent being crowded with ladies, whose native charms and richly tinted summer attire vied with the flushing hues..." The list of the well-to-do was extensive: the Dean of Llandaff; the Rev. Thomas of Llandaff Court; the Bookers; and not a footballer among them.

Another Whitchurch Floral and Horticultural Show was held in June 1847, and again in September of that year, taking place under a marquee at "Wentreoda [sic]", one of the attractions being "a monster rope of onions about ten feet in height, the onions being of splendid growth".

The first show of 1848 went ahead in June, on "the Common at Waintroeda [sic]", and was the "sixth annual spring exhibition of the society", which dates it to 1842. Again the notable guest list was extensive. The second show of the 1848 Whitchurch Floral and Horticultural Society was held in September at Gwauntreoda Common. Although the weather was favourable, the more influential and wealthy of the neighbourhood were not in as great attendance as had been seen previously. That said, the attendance was another list of Who's Who, naming: T.W. Booker; Henry Lewis (Greenmeadow); and Wyndham Lewis (Heath) among the attendees. These shows went on annually and only ended when the patronage of T.W. Booker declined.

One of the more notable visitors was Dr Price of Pontypridd who arrived "on a small chesnut [sic] pony and dressed in his usual ancient and peculiar style. He was accompanied by his daughter on a donkey, a beautiful and interesting little girl of about six or seven years of age, dressed in the ancient costume of the royal court of Glamorgan."

The prize list was extensive, covering just about every vegetable and flower you could think of, and the winners in general seemed to be those who were well connected – those who rubbed shoulders with the great and the good. For most of these events, The Three Elms hosted the dinners, all arranged for the various members of the Society after the show had ended.

It was the June 1849 event during which "a prettily devised plough" was reported (see the 'Whitchurch Common' chapter), a symbol that for generations embodied a prominent social landmark for many locally.

The aforementioned Dr William Price was the man who 'pioneered' cremation. A self-proclaimed Arch Druid, he trained as a doctor at The Royal College of Surgeons, London. When his son died in infancy, he chose to cremate him. He was prosecuted for the act, but was found not guilty, thereby establishing a precedent for legal cremation in Britain.

Following news of his death in January 1893, many people sent letters and telegrams expressing sympathy to the family, one of them a resident of Llandaff Yard who informed the family he had "seen the Hindus and Burmese burn their dead ... and should be quite capable of carrying out the wishes of the late Dr. Price".

He wasn't taken up on the offer.

Local News

I'm just going to include a snapshot of some of the news – or should that be olds? – from Whitchurch's past. Otherwise I'd have to write another book.

These are all quotes from various local newspapers. I have not made reference to the actual newspaper sources, as I think that would be too tedious for you, the reader. You may also have noticed the dodgy spelling and grammar used in some material, but it is all of its time, just as it appeared in the newspapers of the day. I have opted to show it throughout, warts n'all.

Let's start with a feel-good story. There must have been something good in the air in August 1836, because an article appeared in the newspapers about a "curious statistic, in the small parish of Whitchurch, near Cardiff, the following very aged old persons are now living in the Upper Hamlet of that parish:

- Thomas Mathew, labourer, and formerly a lime burner 104 yrs
- Mary Lloyd, farm labourer's widow 86
- Catherine Howell, mother of Lieut. Howell, Royal Navy 96?

- Christopher James, shopkeeper 85
- Mary Edwards, shepherd's widow 89
- William Thomas, roller-man 80
- David Howell, formerly scrap-man, Melin Griffith-Works 83
- Thomas Morgan, civil engineer 87
- Edward John, labourer in husbandry 81
- David Robert, weaver 85

The combined ages of these ten, being 876. There was also a great number between 70 and 80."

Crime and punishment

Of course, then as now, the news was not usually so cheerful, and crime often dominated the headlines. In January 1854, a woman called Ann Davies, alias Welsh Ann, was charged with stealing a quilt and a sheet at Whitchurch; and a man by the name of Llewellyn Thomas was charged with receiving the same, well knowing them to have been stolen. There was no evidence against Ann Davies and she was acquitted. The male prisoner was found guilty and sentenced to one month's imprisonment, with hard labour, at Cardiff.

In April of that year at the Llandaff Petty Sessions, an adjournment was held on the 13th instant when Mary Oldfield, of Whitchurch, attended "to aliate her bastard child" and the magistrates adjudged Thomas Thomas to be the father, ordering him to pay 2s 6d a week from the date of the summons against him, along with 26s costs.

In June 1856 at Cardiff Police Court, James Stevens, a boatman, was charged with having stolen a cheese, "the property of Mr. William Phillips, of Whitchurch", from a cart, which he followed on the Blackweir road. "Mary Evans [A witness] deposed that she lived at Blackweir, and on Friday she saw the prisoner and two other young men running after Mr. Phillips's car, [the] prisoner ran faster than the others, and on overtaking the cart about 70 or 80 yards from her house she [sic] saw him take the cheese out of the cart, and put it under his smock; she called her husband, David Evans, who was in the gardens, and he went out and took the prisoner into custody. William Phillips deposed that he was returning from Cardiff on Friday, and had two cheeses in the cart, he missed one and that was the cheese now produced. [The accused was] Summarily convicted, and sent to prison for two months, with hard labour."

The end of that year, December 1856, saw a spate of poultry rustling. A farm on the Heath "lost seven very excellent geese" in one night from a locked-up shed. In the same week on the Ty Clyd farm (now Whitchurch Hospital), "several ducks were walked off by the marauders". If this had happened in more modern times, we could perhaps have assumed that the perpetrators had been watching the Christmas showing of *Wallace and Gromit*, and had been inspired by the sheep rustling episode...

In January 1862, four men were arrested for committing a burglary with violence at "the house of a respectable elderly couple named Richards, who lived in a house near Whitchurch". One of the men had a pistol and one a dagger and they threatened to murder the occupants, but "all they could find was £3 with which they decamped".

They were apprehended two weeks later, one being a ticket of leave convict – in effect, he was still serving a sentence for a previous crime, but was trusted enough to work outside the prison. I doubt he was granted that kind of liberty again! Three of the four went by the aliases Monsey, Gosling and Hicky Skew. All were well-known characters, apparently; with nicknames like that, what else could they do but follow a life of crime?

In May 1863, "A robbery was effected at Llandaff Railway Station ... a sum upwards of £4 was stolen from the clerk's cash box. The thief affected [sic] his entrance through the door by wresting the iron bar and forcing it out of the socket."

In June 1867, Richard Davis of Whitchurch was summoned for turning out his donkeys on the roads at night to graze. The defendant claimed that they had broken out of their enclosure. He was ordered to pay costs of 7s 3d.

Daniel Llewellyn, also of Whitchurch, was similarly dealt with for the same offence. Coincidentally, or perhaps not, there are no other reports on the famous Whitchurch donkey escapologists.

In July 1893, at the Llandaff justices, two brothers Frank and Harry Stone of Whitchurch were charged with stealing a quantity of apples valued at 2s 6d (12½p now), the property of Mr William Douglas Blessley, at Llanishen. Both prisoners were fined 20s (£1) + costs. If they were unable to pay, they would face 14 days' imprisonment. And if you think that's harsh, in August 1882, Stephen Rice, Joseph Stone and George Hole, all of Whitchurch, were fined, the first two, 2s 6d and Hole 5s, including costs, for playing pitch and toss on the highway. It was Hole's second offence, hence the more severe punishment.

Some victims of crime, coming to the end of their tether, began to hone their own skills as detectives. At Llandaff Police Court in December 1897, William Perry was charged with stealing a jug of jam from the shop of Mr William Evans, a grocer in Whitchurch. The accused was delivering sacks of corn to Mr Evans' shop, and as he was leaving, the grocer, having had things go missing before, noticed something under his apron. Perry received a sentence of 14 days' hard labour.

Spare a thought for a man by the name of Joseph John Stone. Back in October 1906, "At Llandaff Police-court Joseph John Stone was charged with frequenting 'Heldon road' (Heol Don), Whitchurch, on the 11th and 12th inst. [the current month] for the purpose of betting. Police-sergeant Bennett deposed that, about 1.15 p.m. on the 11th he saw the defendant, who had dismounted from a baker's van, take money and slips of paper from eight men. He also on the 12th saw Stone on the same spot take money from four men. Prisoner, who admitted the charge, was fined 20s and costs, or, in default, seven days' imprisonment. The second charge was adjourned for a month." A bit harsh for something which would now be considered as trivial.

It wasn't just adults committing petty crimes. In January 1888, a 13-year-old youth, Richard Thomas, a labourer living in Whitchurch, was charged with stealing 3s (15p now) from the Ton Inn, Tongwynlais. He apparently crept into the bar of the inn and took the money from a saucer, but he was collared by the publican.

"The bench dealing leniently with the prisoner, ordered him to receive 12 strokes with the birch." If that's leniency, I wouldn't have wanted to be on the receiving end of a harsh punishment.

In fact, it wasn't just humans committing crimes. September 1898 saw a Whitchurch rooster attacked by a dog, and the unfortunate victim ended up losing all its tail feathers apart from one. "The owner said that if the vigilance folk will let it [the rooster] live the Cardiff Art Society shall have it as a model for a poster." To promote a 19th-Century punk band, no doubt.

It's a hard life

Working the land was a tough job and accidents were common. In July 1863, "Joseph Hurley, was engaged with a wagon and a team of horses hauling hay for Mrs. Rowland of Treoda Castle ... One of the horses (a restive one) suddenly started off and while attempting to stop them he was struck down by the shaft and the wagon passed over him and broke the thigh bone of one of his legs." He was attended to by the local doctor and a sum of money was collected from his neighbours for him, "which under the circumstances will prove a great boon to the family, who are deserving people".

Accidents with wagons and carts occurred regularly. In March 1886, at half past eight in the morning, Mr Phillips of Wauntreoda Farm was almost killed: "He was riding on the shaft of a cart on his way home from one of the fields and on passing through the gate leading to his house the wheel came into contact with the post and the horse bolted." He was eventually thrown off and "the wheel of the cart passed over his shoulder. He was taken to his house and the doctor sent for ... His injuries were not so serious as might have been the case." At least they were not fatal.

Farm incidents and thefts were many; this one is typical. In November 1881, Ty Clyd Farm lost several sheep, but the culprit was tracked down. A 'huckster' (a pedlar of dubious morals) from the Rhondda Valley was caught with two sheep in his possession when a police sergeant "found several sheep on the road and noticed several marks on the road which aroused his suspicion". Spotting a vehicle (a trap) near the entrance to the farm, he then followed and, after making enquiries, he traced it to Porth where he informed the Rhondda police, resulting in the apprehension of the sheep thief.

It wasn't just working the land that made for a tough life for local people; many things around the parish were harsh too. In January 1876, the Cardiff Rural Sanitary Authority reported that public pumps in Whitchurch and at Llandaff Yard required some repairs. A big concern when it came to land drainage and poor sanitation systems.

"In Whitchurch upwards of 30 houses were in a bad sanitary condition in consequence of the overcharged state of the back offices and the foul state of the ditches. The Inspector therefore recommended that the owner should be called upon to construct proper drains and ash pits."

Poor sanitation was exacerbated by the practice of keeping pigs in sties that had no proper drainage. Near the Long-row, there were two cottages in a state of dilapidation, which rendered them unfit for habitation, and a serious nuisance was caused to these dwellings by the overflow of sewage matter from the Tyn-y-Pwll farm.

However, the medical officer reported, "The health of the district was not unsatisfactory. Scarlet fever existed, but no deaths from this cause had been registered during the past month."

Count your blessings to live in hygienic times. In October 1876, the district medical officer again reported on local health issues relating to sanitary conditions:

"The sanitary state of the cottages at Bridge Row, Whitchurch was sadly deficient. The Ty'n y Coed cottages, Whitchurch, were in a most dilapidated condition and were quite unfit for human habitation. The woman in one of them stated that the children in bed were often saturated by the water coming through the roof during wet weather."

The inspector for the north district reported that Ty'n y Coed cottages were unfit for human habitation and steps were taken to close them and the Bridge Row cottages while "measures were being taken to get them efficiently drained".

Look away now if you are squeamish or preparing food... In November of 1881, there was a case against Solomon Andrews, a man with an immense reputation in Cardiff, brought by the Cardiff Rural Sanitary Authority's Medical Officer, who complained of a nuisance caused by Mr Andrews at the Great House Farm, Whitchurch:

"To this place all the old, diseased, and worn-out horses owned by Mr Andrews were sent from Cardiff, where they died or were killed, and their carcases allowed to remain on the ground without being buried, and the pigs, which were intended for human food, ran about and ate the carcases all up."

The authority ordered the inspector (of Health) to take out a summons against Mr Andrews at once.

In February 1884, the Rural Sanitary Authority held a monthly meeting to discuss many district issues, among which the medical officer reported a nuisance on Ty'n y Cae Farm, Whitchurch. One of the outbuildings was used as a slaughterhouse and the "refuse from the 'killing of the beasts' flowed into the yard and when this overflowed, into a brook by the side of the yard, the water from which was used for drinking purposes by the villagers". Of all the things to have to contend with. Needless to say, an immediate stop was imposed.

In August 1876, there was a terrific storm: "In a field between Heol Don and Merthyr Road several sheep, the property of Mr Thomas Williams, Ty Clyd Farm, were sheltering under a tree, when suddenly seven were killed by a flash of lightning, which also threw down about four feet of the edge wall, made a rent in the edge, scarred the bark on the bottom of the tree and left a sulphurous appearance and odour thereon. Some wool was forcibly torn off the sheep's body and conveyed several feet up the trunk of the tree and a great portion of the leaves were scorched."

I wonder if you have ever thought of salaries of those times. In March 1878, there were two candidates for the office of registrar of births and deaths at Whitchurch, said to be worth about £20 a year. It became "vacant by the death of the last incumbent and Mr Hopkins, relieving officer, was elected, no one proposed the other candidate". Mr Hopkins, registrar, lived on the Philog.

The 19th Century in Whitchurch brought tough times indeed, and some people became desperate enough to turn to crime, especially when they had children to care for. In November 1889, Rose Reed, a married woman residing with her husband in Whitchurch, was charged with stealing two pairs of baby's shoes from a trap on the road. At the time of the theft, she had a child in her arms. Perhaps she thought being the mother of an infant made her beyond the reach of the law; if so, she was wrong. She was "bound over in two sureties of £5 each to appear for judgement when called upon", which must have been a bitter pill to swallow if she couldn't even afford clothing for her child.

The mystery of the miller

Here's a curious story from 1891. You may have heard of a dead man walking, but what about a dead man reading?

In September of that year, the *Cardiff Times* headlined a "SUDDEN DEATH AT WHITCHURCH". The report went on to state:

"An inquest touching the death of Henry Bate, miller, Whitchurch, was conducted at the Birch-Grove public house, Whitchurch, on Friday by Mr Reece, coroner, when the following evidence was taken.

"—Eliza Bate, widow of the deceased, living at 3, Windmill Cottages, Whitchurch, said her husband was 59 years of age. He had not been well for some time, but had been able to follow his work. He suffered from bronchitis during the winter, but never complained of this until after they had gone to live in a new house.

"She last saw him alive on Tuesday, the 8th inst., when he set off to his work at the Derry Mill. On that day she went to stay with some friends at Cardiff, and on her return about 5 p.m. on the 9th inst., she found her husband sitting dead in his chair with his arms leaning across the table. He had apparently just been having tea, as the tea things were on the table.

"She called a neighbour, Mrs Nicholas, to come in, and she found him quite cold. He had not been to work that day, nor had the bed been slept in. She thought he must have died just after tea on Tuesday night.

"—Jane Nicholas, who lived next door, said she saw the deceased about half-past eight on the Tuesday. He was sitting at the table with a lamp in front of him reading a letter. She saw him in this position through the window. She noticed that the tea things were also on the table. She saw him in the same place about an hour afterwards, but he was not reading, and appeared to be asleep. On Wednesday, when called to go into the house by Mrs Bate, she found the deceased in exactly the same position. He was then quite cold and stiff. She had never heard him complain, but noticed his breathing was heavy at times.

"—Dr Hardyman said he had seen the body there [sic] were no marks of injury upon it. The evidence pointed to sudden heart failure. He did not think there was anything suspicious about the case."

Evidently, the deceased's mother died in a similar way, and a verdict of death from natural causes was returned.

I'm curious about the name of the cottages in which Mr and Mrs Bate and their neighbour lived, and by the deceased's profession. Who knows of a windmill in Whitchurch? It seems that Wind-mill Cottages would have been in the Pantbach Road area, possibly somewhere between the Birchgrove pub and the Deri, but I have no idea why they are so named.

It's not such a hard life

We've had a look at the hardships suffered by working people of Whitchurch back in the 19th Century, but there were some jobs that were very much sought after. In a magistrate's court in August 1892, expert analysts pondered over the quality of a Whitchurch publican's cwrw (beer), one suggesting it was strongly impregnated with salt (supposedly to make drinkers thirsty), the other denying it. A party of locals complained that such decisions were always left to analysts and offered, free of charge, to form a committee to test all the "liquor in Cardiff and the suburbs". If it hadn't been so long ago, I would be sure I know those men!

Despite the risks and dangers of working on the land, farming in the Whitchurch area was certainly profitable, the fertility of the soil in this area being legendary. In November 1892, the *South Wales Daily News* lauded the success of that year's crop:

"The neighbourhood of Cardiff has again this year proved its right to be considered as possessing some of the best soil for the growth of roots in the whole of the United Kingdom ... Mr. Baker of the Forest Farm, near Whitchurch, has a field which is spoken of as being something extraordinary."

However, while Whitchurch of the past may have a bucolic image for some, the reality was a lot different. Some wealthy families had it good for sure, but for many, it was a life of struggle and hard graft.

Part of this was due to the difficulties faced by the Melingriffith Works in November 1892 when the Whitchurch Distress Committee was busy dispensing relief.

"A large supply of soup was provided by a local grocer and a Mrs Ingledew of Ty'n y Parc, which was distributed to those who applied for it."

The local branch of the Tinplate Workers Union also came to the rescue and distributed £48 to members of the Union. Each man was given 7s 6d and boys 3s 9d (37½ p and 19p in today's money).

Then as now

The state of our 21st-century roads is a constant talking point – perhaps we should invite the Romans back, as their roads have lasted for two millennia. However, as we saw in the 'A Bus Terminus' chapter, these types of complaints are nothing new in Whitchurch.

In December 1894, a local resident saw fit to write to the papers about the road from the Philog to the Birchgrove, then called Philog Road, now called Birchgrove Road (both signs are still visible):

"We don't dare go out of doors after dark at night without being four inches deep in mud or clay!"

Some things never change. The roads were no better by January 1904. One issue faced by Whitchurch Parish Council was:

"...some of the roads in the parish are in an extremely bad state ... there are certain thoroughfares at Whitchurch crying aloud for completion, all the more so because the houses bordering on them have been erected and tenanted for some years." The headline "Bad Roads at Whitchurch" returned in December 1906, flooding being the main issue this time, and that brings us neatly on to our next story.

Here is one for the weather watchers. In January 1903, Whitchurch experienced some extreme weather. A few weeks earlier, heavy rains had caused the brook to flood and "many of the fields between Beulah and the village were submerged". Before the waters had time to fully disperse, there was a heavy frost and a "stretch covering about two acres had frozen to a good thickness and affords splendid skating. The surface is all that can be desired and as the depth of the water is only about 2ft., no fear of danger need be entertained. The field is near the Fox and Hounds Hotel and can be reached from the bus in about three minutes."

The moral of the story? Bad weather isn't always bad news.

All of this chapter has been a snapshot of another age, part of life's rich tapestry. It provides us with a glimpse of how things were in the community at that time, both by the written word and the nature of each event itself.

Whitchurch Pigs

Throughout the land, there are many regional nicknames for people from a particular neck of the woods. Older Whitchurch residents might remember the pig farms in Taffs Well and Radyr, leading to us being affectionately known as the Whitchurch Pigs.

Don't be offended, the term is perfectly respectable. The Whitchurch connection with its pigs lasted for generations and the reputation was both well-earned and held with pride. The nickname came about not just because of the number of people who owned or farmed pigs, but the quality of the breed and, of course, the bacon and ham they produced.

There were many benefits of having pigs, apart from the ready and sustainable supply of meat and a good friendship with the local butcher. They could quickly dispose of any organic waste from the kitchen, and while foraging in the fields, they helped to fertilise the soil and break up the surface layers, providing a simple and instant ploughing system and a regenerative impact on the land without too much work. As children, we were told a number of times, "They'll eat anything, mon!" and "You can eat every part of a pig".

One way local people overcame the cost burden of pig ownership was to form a sort of workers' cooperative in which reliable groups contributed to a fund and bought their pigs as and when they had sufficient money to do so. This procedure made the newspapers in March 1810 and was no doubt copied and repeated as a result by other enterprising people.

> *Pig Club.*—In the parish of Whitchurch, near Cardiff, about forty persons have associated for the purchase of pigs. They subscribe weekly a shilling each, draw lots every Friday night, and on Saturday the fortunate member goes to market with his forty shillings and buys his pig. This plan is pursued till each person has obtained one of those useful animals, which is effected by a weekly susbcription so small as scarcely to be felt in the poorest family.

The Cambrian, 17 March 1810

In December 1830, a report stated that "a pig club had been established at Whitchurch, near Cardiff, by the labouring class of the parish, for the purchase of a pig each for their winter stock, which continues to the present time. The members have taken great pains in the selection of the breed of that useful animal, by crossing the Berkshire with the Glamorgan, and Mr. Edmund Lewis, of Derry Farm, the president for the present year, gained one of Sir Charles Morgan's Cups at his annual show."

Another report that must be mentioned is this, dated January 1832: "An enormous animal bred and fed by Mrs. Lewis, Derry Farm, Whitchurch [those Lewises get everywhere], a pig supposed to be the fattest slaughtered in this county for some years. The following are the dimensions, weight &c., length from snout to the root of the tail 6ft 9ins; girth 6ft 2ins; around the neck 5ft; from snout to forehead 7ins; height to top of shoulder 2ft 10ins; girth on leg bone $6^{7}/_{8}$ ins. Weight 29 'score' 2lbs." A score was 20, so it was probably 582 lbs. Evidently, fully grown pigs can weigh between 110 and 770 lbs. No off-the-shelf, artificially coloured products from unknown suppliers wrapped in cling film in those days, this was grass roots food stock.

In February 1846: "Two pigs, about 20 months old, belonging to Mr. David Thomas, Gwaelod y- Garth Inn, Pentyrch, were slaughtered. One of them weighed 24 score and 16 pounds, and the other 34 score and 6 pounds. These animals were fed solely upon grains until the 20th Nov last, when they were turned in for fattening. They were of the pure Glamorgan breed, reared from an old stock in the parish of Whitchurch, a place celebrated for the superiority of its breed of pigs."

As you might imagine, pig theft (pig-napping?) wasn't uncommon, some cases ending up in court when the owners tracked their animals down, with a police escort. In the homes of suspects, sometime their neighbours, who'd been selling joints of meat, they'd find the butchered carcasses hanging as evidence.

It wasn't a case of owning a pig anywhere, as you would a pet. Some fell foul of the law, being charged with keeping swine within the District of the Cardiff Health Board, and were ordered to remove them. No doubt this law was imposed by a covenant, driven by health and hygiene.

In October 1866, several incidents were brought to the bench. A man by the name of Richard Davis was summoned for keeping four pigsties close to his premises at Whitchurch. He was ordered to remove them and pay costs. William Stephens of Albert Cottages, Whitchurch (where were they? I wonder) was summoned for having two pigsties close to his dwelling house, along with a donkey house, a goose house and sundry vessels containing a stinking pigwash. He was ordered to remove the sties and pay costs – the pigwash must have been acceptable. His next-door neighbour Daniel Roberts was summoned for exactly the same thing, with the same decision given.

Daniel Morgan was summoned "for having a foul pigstye on the highway at Whitchurch. He was ordered to remove it and pay 5s 9d + costs." Daniel Thomas of Elm Cottage, Whitchurch was similarly dealt with for the same issue – was it a Daniel thing?

A father and son – both named John, not Daniel – were given a fine and ordered to pay court costs for keeping two pigs and a heap of manure on the highway at Whitchurch – poor crop of rhubarb that year, obviously. William Porter, summoned for having several pigsties and nearly 20 pigs close to his dwelling at Whitchurch, was ordered to pay costs and remove them, while William Thomas and

Edward Edwards were both fined one shilling and costs for keeping pigs in a filthy state at Whitchurch.

In December 1872, David Lewis (it's that name again), a labourer at Whitchurch, was summoned for allowing two pigs to stray on the highway. The wife of the defendant appeared, and a police constable stationed at Whitchurch gave evidence. The defendant's wife apparently did not deny the charge, but she did consider that the police were partial, as other persons' pigs were allowed to stray, and the police took no notice of them. She even gave a name, but the police constable denied this statement, and the magistrate fined her 10s and costs.

On leaving the box, Mrs Lewis muttered something, and the magistrate said, "What is that?" The police constable replied that she'd said it was a scandalous shame, for which the fine was changed to 20s and costs. The woman left the court, complaining of the harshness of the Bench.

Swine fever

These were not the only problems owning pigs came with. In August 1882, a case of swine fever was reported in Tongwynlais and Whitchurch, which would have caused devastation to the owners. It was reported: "Swine fever is often spread by pigs taken from a place where one or two animals have died from the disease to the market and there sold, as many people would rather [do this] than inform the authorities." In March 1883, William Steel, a farmer in Llandaff Yard, was fined £5 plus costs for not notifying the police that four of his pigs were suffering from swine fever.

In June 1884, the harrowing news came that swine fever had again hit the area, having previously "played such havoc in this neighbourhood ... On Saturday morning Mr. George Steele of the Crown Inn, Llandaff Yard, was obliged to destroy six valuable pigs which had been attacked."

In October 1886, the world and his wife knew that Richard Wadley's farm at "Tynycae, Whitchurch ... in the petty sessional division of Kibbor, Glamorganshire, which were declared to be areas infected with swine fever, are declared to be free from swine fever". This was a relief to him no doubt, but the reputation would have tainted his pigs for quite some time afterwards in the marketplace.

The news was not so good for our village in November 1889. The *London Gazette* contained a report issued by the Board of Agriculture: "The area comprising the petty sessional division of Kibbor, in the county of Glamorgan, was declared, by privy council order of October 3rd 1887, to be infected with swine fever, is now free from such infection, with the exception of the parish of Whitchurch."

It lingered. In June 1896, the wholesale destruction of pigs took place at Whitchurch due to the reappearance of swine fever. It did not end there, either. There were many more reports in June 1898 and August 1899, and swine fever spread to wider areas. It was still a problem in 1905. It certainly makes you think twice before taking a chance of having pigs on your allotment.

Bacon galore

I have to tell you one more story before we leave this chapter. Many of you will know of the book and film *Whisky Galore*, where local people on a tiny Scottish island went to great lengths to conceal their stash of illegally obtained whisky. Well, in the mid- to late-19th Century, the authorities sent a small group of officials to Whitchurch, having heard that many families were keeping pigs illegally and leaving them to roam freely to forage. Word got around that these officials were on their way, and as they approached the target homes, the locals set about moving the pigs around from place to place to avoid detection, hiding them in houses, sheds, outhouses, the Ty-bach and even under the bed, staying one step ahead. Not one single pig was found and the officials went away completely baffled.

Bacon sandwich, anyone?

Whitchurch Parish Council

A meeting of the parish council was held in August 1898. Among the topics on the agenda was the state of the roads, some houses near Ty'n y Coed being "without a proper water supply" and some in the Upper Village (the Fox and Hounds area) having "not been properly drained". The minutes also stated that "the county council be asked to erect a police station at Whitchurch".

In October 1900, the parish council accepted reports that the diversion of the old tithe barn path from Heol Don had been satisfactorily concluded. At the same meeting, it was decided that wicket gates would be placed in several important places in the parish. It's only recently (sadly) that the last of these gates has been removed.

There is a not too complimentary account from January 1904. Headlined "Whitchurch Parish Emblem", it went on to state, "Ever since the village of Whitchurch has been a village, the natives have been called 'Whitchurch pigs,' on account, it is supposed, of the villagers fattening and curing their own bacon. Now, residents prefer to buy Wiltshire best smoked, or some other brand. As a consequence, the cognomen 'Whitchurch pigs' has almost vanished. But, the village election artist appears determined that the euphonious title shall be revived. His latest production is a 'coat of arms,' which, as he sarcastically puts it, won the handsome prize of 4d, offered by the parish council, for the best design submitted to them for an appropriate embellishment to the now free library buildings. The 'prize' sketch proudly showed the pig in the centre of a shield, a fat Berkshire, ready, as it were, for the knife. On the top of the shield is the head of one of the Glamorgan species (for it has good long ears) with outstretched wings attached. The artist's idea in including a flying pig in his design is not very clear; but he may have concluded, perhaps, that it would be well to arrange to place the free library on wheels, so that it could be shifted periodically from one part of the parish to the other. The sketch has caused some amusement, but everyone is asking what it means. The only one who can reply is the election artist."

No doubt, after being likened to fattened pigs, the parish councillors would have scripted a strong reply, whether their library plans were realistic or not.

The Coryton Railway

The writing was on the wall for the Glamorganshire Canal (see the 'Places of Note' chapter) when the iron masters and coal owners started to demand a more efficient transport system to get their products to market and wider distribution. As early as November 1834, the Merthyr Tydfil and Cardiff Railway posted notice of intent of plans to construct a new route, which turned out to be the same Taff Vale Railway (T.V.R.) that we have today. This was the exact wording of the company's statement:

"NOTICE IS HEREBY GIVEN that application is intended to be made to Parliament in the next Session for leave to bring in a Bill to make and maintain a Railway with proper works and conveniences connected therewith, commencing at or near an open space of ground, on the south side of the town of Merthyr Tydfil, lying between the River Taff and the Turnpike-road leading from Merthyr Tydfil to Cardiff." In doing so, the Merthyr Tydfil and Cardiff Railway virtually secured a monopoly on rail transport through the Taff valley, the geology of which created pinch points at a few locations, restricting the possibility of an alternative transport system.

As a direct result of the commercial rivalry this created, in July 1897, plans were underway by the Bute Docks Company, which shortly after changed its name to the Cardiff Railway Company, to construct a railway line. It was to run from a junction at Llanishen to Pontypridd and form a junction with the Taff Vale Railway at Treforest, communicating directly with the coalfields in the Rhondda and Aberdare Valleys. This branch was intended for minerals only, with stations proposed at Whitchurch, Tongwynlais, Upper Boat and the northern terminus.

Although this railway was completed, the plans to converge with the Taff Vale Railway could not go any further, due to the Merthyr Tydfil and Cardiff Railway purchasing a strategic plot of land near Treforest, thereby preventing any possibility of them linking up. The Cardiff Railway Company continued not to have an easy time of things. The public right of way was a big issue, particularly to farm owners and people who relied on ancient footpaths and tracks to go about their daily business. Whitchurch Parish Council met in August 1898 and approved the diversion of a footpath in Llanishen after the Cardiff Railway had amended its scheme.

In February 1899 at a "lively meeting of ratepayers", the parish council had a busy time with an item on the railway once again on the agenda. After some discussion, it was resolved to call the attention of district and parish councillors to the proposals of the Cardiff Railway

Company to cross Mr Wadley's field, asking that they use every legitimate means to persuade the company to discontinue the obstruction which would be caused by the chosen path of the track.

In March 1899, however, "The diversion of a footpath by the Cardiff Railway Company between the upper village [Whitchurch] and Beulah Chapel, Whitchurch came on for discussion at the Whitchurch Parish Council." The line passed over the footpath and the company proposed to provide a bridge to carry the line over the brook. But the levels made it impracticable to construct the bridge. The company had given an undertaking to purchase the necessary land and make an additional footpath 6 feet wide parallel to the line and provide a level crossing with gates to carry the existing footpath over the line. This, however, did "not meet with the views of the parishioners who want a proper footbridge erected or a new footpath made that will be as convenient as the present footpath". All this was behind the design and construction of the bridge and footpaths we have today.

The train and the tithe barn

You will likely know of the tithe barn near The Hollybush, once part of the village landscape. The remains of its foundations now lie under the entry / exit road to Clos Coed Hir, on the edge of the old Whitchurch Hospital site.

Its fate was sealed in February 1900, when shortly before ten on a Tuesday morning, it was found on fire. Two police constables and members of the Whitchurch fire brigade attended with fire appliances, but the barn, which had a thatched roof and contained a large quantity of straw, could not be saved. The fire was supposedly "caused by a spark from a passing locomotive".

The railway the locomotive was running on was what we now know as the Coryton line. Trains at that time were steam-powered and coal-fuelled. Older residents with good memories will remember the trains' funnels discharging thick grey-black smoke, as well as airborne cinders and sparks that often set alight the dry vegetation alongside the tracks on warm, dry days.

It's a wonder that no one saw it coming that one day, the sparks would set more than the vegetation alight.

Buildings of Interest

Ty Mawr

Ty Mawr – 'Great House' – on Westbourne Crescent is a grade II listed building dating from the 16th Century, although it has been modernised over the years. It is believed to be the earliest dated house that survives in Glamorgan – 1583 – but very little of the original building remains.

A couple of centuries after it was built, it was the home of Anthony Mathew, a kinsman of the earl and agent for the Llandaff Estate, who died c.1825 without issue and intestate, unusual for a member of the Mathew family, it being a name with a deep-rooted pedigree and traceable to many of the ancient manors in the region, notably at Llandaff, Radyr and Pentyrch.

The house went up for sale by auction in January 1826: "On the Premises, at the GREAT HOUSE FARM, in the parish of Whitchurch, situate between Mellin Griffith and Cardiff, on Wednesday the 1st day of February, 1826, and following days, – All the valuable LIVE and DEAD FARMING STOCK, IMPLEMENTS of HUSBANDRY, HOUSE-HOLD FURNITURE, and other EFFECTS of the late Mr. ANTHONY

MATHEWS, deceased. The Farming Stock consists of six milch cows, three fat cows, four fat oxen, four four-year-old working ditto, four three-year-old ditto, four two-year old, and two yearling cattle 38 fat sheep, 3 ewes, two rams, and 28 lambs; four fat pigs four cart and two saddle horses three ricks of wheat, a large quantity of barley in the straw, and four large ricks of hay; three wagons, four carts, and a variety of ploughs, harrows, drags, rollers, drill machines, winnowing machines, hurdles, bags, &c..

"The Household Furniture comprises a general assortment of excellent and useful articles, kitchen requisites, and dairy and brewing utensils."

The sale included other land, as well as: "The GREAT HOUSE FARM, containing by estimation 125 Acres, more or less, of most excellent Arable and Pasture Land, will be Let by Private Contract, for one year, from 2nd February; the wheat in the ground, manure, ploughing, &c. to be taken at a fair valuation, by the in-coming tenant, and eight months' credit will be given for the same on approved security.

"GELLY FARM, adjoining Great House Farm, containing about 30 Acres, more or less, will be let on the same condition on application to Mr. Wm. Mathews, on the premises."

Clearly, Anthony Mathew left an extensive and rich estate by anyone's standards.

In April 1831, a barn belonging to Mr Evan Rees suffered a freak accident when it was struck by lightning: "A farmer residing at Great House, Whitchurch, about three miles from Cardiff, was struck by 'the electric fluid' and a quantity of wheat and potatoes consumed, with the rapidity of the flash by which it was ignited. Fortunately seven fine cows which were usually kept in the barn had been taken out to be milked just before."

Ty Mawr and its lands were placed up for auction again in March 1854: "On the Premises, at the Great House Farm, in the Parish of Whitchurch, Glamorganshire, on TUESDAY Next, the 14th day of March, 1854,— THE whole of the excellent Live and Dead STOCK of Mr. Thomas Purnell, who is retiring from farming pursuits. The Great House Farm is within a few hundred yards of the Llandaff Station of the Taff Vale Railway."

There was another fire in February 1857, this time affecting a different property owner. You are likely to recognise his name.

"About mid-day on Wednesday last a fire was perceived to issue from a barn near the Great House Farm, Whitchurch, the property of T.W. Booker Blakemore, Esq., M.P. An account of the accident was sent to Mr. Thomas, the manager of the Melin Griffith Works, who promptly dispatched a number of workmen to the scene of danger, but the fire had by this time gained too great an ascendency to be suppressed, and the building together with a wagon and other articles belonging to Mr. R. Lougher, who is the occupier of the farm, were destroyed, but by the united efforts of the Melin Griffith workmen the valuable property in the rick yard was saved."

The fire started after a spark from the railway carried through the wind and ignited the barn.

In 1888, following the death of T.W. Booker (the son), all Ty Mawr assets were sold off. These included the Melingriffith Works as well as various large farms and hereditaments that were the property of the Cardiff Iron and Tin Plate Co Ltd, which was at the time in liquidation. The list was impressive, one item being The Gwaelod y Garth Inn:

"Also, the Valuable Melin Griffith Iron and Tin Plate Works together with the Freehold and Leasehold Lands and Cottage held therewith, consisting of the Leckwith Woods, 40 Freehold Cottages, 13 Leasehold Cottages, Freehold Ochre Works and Garden, and Part of the Freehold Great House Farm, in the Parish of Whitchurch. The whole of the foregoing will be sold in convenient lots."

This signalled the beginning of the end for Ty Mawr. From this point onwards, the house and farm parted company, the latter being divided into lots and sold off.

Ty Mawr lends its name to Ty Mawr Road, which follows the route of the old Glamorganshire Canal. It lies at the bottom of the sloping lane just off Westbourne Crescent as it drops down on to Ty Mawr Road. The lane has now been fashioned into a series of steps and a chicane to prevent young cyclists recklessly belting down it at a rate of knots, as they did in the 1950s and 60s.

Island Cottage

Island Cottage is a building of open and hidden character. Located at the gateway to our village, now the home of a funeral director, it lies alongside the brook, and in its past lay between the brook and a millstream (leat) that channelled water to Little Mill (Felin Fach), 400 metres away. The remains of the weir that diverted the brook water are still there.

On the 1840 tithe map, the cottage was occupied by a John Williams and the land was owned by Lord Dynevor, who owned large areas of the region. By March 1884 it was occupied by Mrs Mary Powell, but because she was "giving up house-keeping", she put the contents up for sale. This tends to suggest that she was not the owner of the property. Possibly, due to her age, she was leaving to live elsewhere, perhaps with a son or a daughter, but that is pure conjecture.

The interest here is that the contents of her home make for a good insight into not just her lifestyle, but also the cottage itself. From the description of the contents, "Sale of First Class Household Furniture &c, &c.", you might conclude that she was a woman of some standing. Much of her furniture was mahogany, as was a "capital piano (Broadwood)", and her sitting room included two eight-day clocks, a barometer, glass decanters, wine glasses, ornaments and a quantity of books. Clearly, she was someone with taste, as well as a decent level of education, something that was not common at that time.

Her bedroom furniture included a half-tester tent (a canopy over the head end of the bed), a mahogany commode (where else could you go in the middle of the night when it was dark?) and a new shower bath. There would not have been a supply of fresh water back in the day and no piped waste system. Guess what the convenient water supply and disposal facility would have been.

The kitchen makes for interesting reading. Apart from the utensils you would expect, there were two steelyard scales and weights (see below), and a gun. The list also included "brewing utensils, casks, tubs and vats, garden tools and pig troughs". Of value and considered worthy of the sale were "several splendid hams and sides of home-cured bacon". You can build your own picture from this.

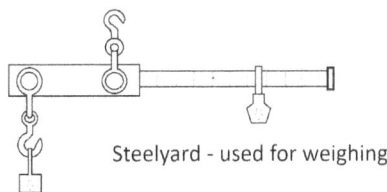

Steelyard - used for weighing

In the early days of the cottage, there was no footbridge over the brook; there was a ford, used for farm vehicles and livestock to travel between the old farm and mill, Felin Fach and the Merthyr Road, with the trail leading from the ford along a lane, which still exists, to what is now Ty Newydd.

For some of us, there is a memory of a dear old woman who stood regularly at that front door when we were children, offering a friendly wave and a delicate smile, dressed in a pinny and ankle-length dress. The door of Island Cottage through the 1960s always had a sandbag in front of it because of flooding from the brook, which was just feet away. You can bet that the building had a flagstone floor at ground level for that very reason, which is probably still intact.

The Willows

This house, now replaced by a more modern apartment block, stood close to the old church, on a triangular piece of land between the Fox and Hounds pub and The Pines. In August 1910, it was advertised To Let, described as a "Charming Detached Residence; four reception, six bed rooms; conservatory; garden; stable; coach house; station ten minutes".

Some older neighbouring residents, when they were children, used to refer to it as the old vicarage, a suggestion, perhaps, as to what it once was in its earliest days.

Whitchurch Vicarage

On 8 August 1845, Whitchurch was converted from a chapelry to a separate independent parish, of which the Bishop of Llandaff was patron. On 22 October that same year, the Rev. Evan Price Thomas became the first Vicar of the Parish of Whitchurch, a post he held until his retirement towards the end of 1868. Prior to this, he seems to have been one of the vicars of Llandaff since 1843, and he continued to serve Llandaff as well as Whitchurch until 1857.

During the time of the Rev. E.P. Thomas, there was a considerable growth of population in the parish, due mainly to the Melingriffith and Pentyrch works. The estimated population of the parish at the time of his retirement was 2,274.

The *Directory for Bristol and Glamorgan, 1865*, wrote of the Parish of Whitchurch: "The church stands in the village but is destitute of any important feature. It is a low structure without tower, surrounded by a pretty graveyard. The interior will be entirely renovated and reseated during the summer at considerable cost. The living is a perpetual curacy, value £80 per annum, in the patronage of the Bishop of Llandaff and held by Rev. Evan Price Thomas. A neat parsonage house is in course of erection."

The parsonage house referred to here is the vicarage in Penlline Road. Improvements followed and in 1874, it was reported that, "The greater part of the interior has been renovated and a handsome parsonage built." Although the precise date of the vicarage is not given, it seems reasonable to assume that it was completed in or around 1866, the report coming some years later.

Originally, the land / garden surrounding the vicarage was extensive, so much so that it hosted many local events. Among these were eisteddfodau, horticultural shows and suppers. The Whitchurch and District Horticultural Society held its first show on the vicarage field in August 1906 with "a large number of entries" and hosted "a party of blind people from the Cardiff Institution". The Whitchurch Brass Band played a selection of music and the local male voice choir sang on the occasion. The event also offered a "good programme of sports" with a large number of competitors having entered.

The third show of the Society was held in August 1908, with some notable attendees. The opening ceremony was performed by the Lord Mayor of Cardiff (Alderman Illtyd Thomas) and the luncheon which followed was presided over by Mr J. Herbert Cory supported by Colonel Henry Lewis (Greenmeadow) among others. "Indeed the exhibition was far and away the best ever held under the society's auspices."

An eisteddfod held in July 1907 proved to be a popular event, attracting competitors from a wide area. The tenor and soprano solos were won by people from Abertillery; the contralto solo by someone from Treorchy; the pianoforte solo by a competitor from Griffithstown; the winning male voice choir was from Treorchy; the winning mixed choir was from Tonyrefail; and the tug-of-war was won by the Cardiff

City Police. The adjudicators in this last contest were, coincidentally, Inspector Nott and Sergeant Bennett of Glamorgan Constabulary.

Woollen factory

In June 1869, it was announced that "a 'Woollen Manufactory' is to be built which when completed will give employment to from 60 to 80 hands, including men, women and children". Although no name was mentioned, it was to be built by "a native of this place who is now in connection with a well known Merthyr woollen manufacturer".

It is not too difficult to work out who it was. The old maps of 1875 show the woollen factory near The Mason's Arms on land owned by John Homfray Esq. The Homfrays were successful ironmasters with works around Merthyr and Ebbw Vale, so there's little doubt he's our man.

John Homfray married Ann Maria, the daughter of the agent of the Marquess of Bute, reportedly the richest man in the world at the time.

The buildings described in this section all played an important part in the history of our village. If you have any memories of them yourself or those passed down from the older generations of your family, treasure them and hang on to them. Tell the stories of the past to your own children and grandchildren; some of these buildings may be gone, but let's not allow them to be forgotten.

The Church

We are all aware of the village centre and the general layout around the Main Road (or Merthyr Road, never High Street as some non-locals like to call it), but Church Road was one of the later additions. In October 1881 at a monthly meeting of the Llandaff Highway Board, a letter was read from the vicar of Whitchurch, asking if the board would contribute something towards a new route leading from the Merthyr Turnpike Road near the Plough Inn in the Parish of Whitchurch, straight to the Llandaff Station T.V.R.

In April 1882, the board announced that it had decided to contribute £130 towards the cost of making the new road and that the T.V.R. Company had promised an additional £20. In July of the same year, news came that construction was to start on the new road and the land on each side "will be most eligible for the erection of respectable villas" as "there is very great demand for respectable residences in this very healthy locality".

The old parish church (Old Church Road)

This church was not just old, but ancient, believed to date from the 16th Century. Between 1536 and 1540, the

Crown seized and closed down religious establishments in England and Wales, including abbeys, priories, convents and friaries, driven by King Henry VIII's declaration of himself as the Supreme Head of the Church of England. This era was known as the Dissolution of the Monasteries.

At some time in the 16th Century, a new church was built, from which the Welsh name *Egluis Newith (Eglwys Newydd)* was used c.1536 to refer to the location of the so-called castle at Treoda on the east part of the church. The timeline is not clear, though; a study of old photographs indicates that the large south porch was constructed earlier than the main structure, which suggests that the original church possibly dated from the 15th Century. Some believe that it was probably rebuilt in the 17th Century, retaining the original porch, while its dedication to St Mary is believed to be from the 15th Century.

It was not until 1616 that Bishop Godwin confirmed a licence for the celebration of christenings, marriages and burials at the chapel. This is the probable date when the old churchyard came into use, but the oldest gravestone was dated 1697.

In an essentially Welsh-speaking area, the English ministrations were pointless. Few could understand them and in 1662, parishioners complained about services not being in their native tongue. The Bishop conceded to a certain extent and, with what seems to be just a gesture, instructed his chaplains to perform Welsh services in the

Ladies' Chapel. This chapel could be a reference to the old St Mary's here in Whitchurch, but there is a Ladies' Chapel in Llandaff itself, so this isn't known for sure.

It was not always a case of strict pious observance of their duties on the part of the clergy. On 30 June 1663: "The same time and place the said lord Bishop of Landaffe decreed Thomas Griffith Clarke curate of Whitchurch to be suspended *abofficio et beneficio durante beneplacito* [from office and privilege] for his excesse of drunknes in Cardiffe." Then as now, it seems the church could be under scrutiny.

From the 1760s, Whitchurch started to change, due entirely to the development of the Melingriffith Works leading to a rapid increase in the population. For this reason, the need arose to increase the size of the old church. In 1784, a gallery was erected inside, which added extra accommodation, and in about 1810, the chapel underwent a "thorough repair". In May 1863, Thomas William Booker the younger (see the 'Booker and Velindre' chapter) and Mr Barry Wride became churchwardens with the expectation that "several improvements will be affected in the Church, which are much needed".

Something that must be mentioned is an ancient Welsh custom. This was published in March 1834:

"At Whitchurch, near Cardiff, about forty years ago, for a time immemorial previous to that period, on Easter Monday it was usual that every married woman who had never been blessed with issue should repair to the churchyard, being first duly provided with two dozen tennis-balls, one dozen of which were covered with white and the other dozen with black leather; these were cast by the fair votaress over the church from the back ground, and scrambled for by the populace who assembled for that purpose in front of the edifice. So imperative was this custom, that neither rank nor age was excused, until they were relieved by the birth of a child."

Between 1813 and 1849, infant mortality was "very heavy". Large numbers of babies died before reaching 1 year of age, and much larger numbers failed to reach the age of 5.

By 1865 the writing was on the wall for the old church, when it was described as being "destitute of any important feature". In 1875, the Rev. J.T. Clarke became the vicar, coinciding with a huge population change in the parish due to the burgeoning success of the Melingriffith Works. Along with him came the call to seek new accommodation.

In March 1878, the Rev. Clarke issued an appeal for aid in the restoration of the parish church: "The old building is by far too small and most inconvenient for the accommodation of the congregation and besides, a great portion of it is in a most ruinous and sadly dilapidated state."

The diocesan architect, Mr Prichard, went further: "The existing church is not only out of repair, but it is notoriously inadequate in size, is utterly devoid of any ecclesiastical or architectural propriety and is the only one left in the district of this deplorable description." The Rector of Merthyr did not hesitate to stigmatise the old building as the ugliest he had ever seen.

A new church was the answer, one that would accommodate 400 at a cost estimated at £3,000 including all fittings. At that time, the population of the parish was "upwards of 3,000" with most said to "live by their daily labour" and so it was necessary to "look far beyond the parish for the assistance necessary to carry this most desirable object into effect [ie build the new church]".

Prior to this, in November 1876, as a consequence of the overcrowded state of the churchyard, the parish officials considered closing the ground for internments. The Ecclesiastical Commissioners gave a grant of 2 acres of land, conveniently situated in the centre of the village, for building a new church and an additional burial ground. Mrs T.W. Booker laid the first stone of the boundary wall for the new church, but there was no ceremony; only the Rev. Clarke and one or two others were present. This is now the site of St Mary's Church on Penlline Road.

The 1880s signalled the end of our old parish church. The ancient structure had been poorly maintained and by 1883, it was described as "small and dilapidated". At the same time as the new St Mary's Church was being built, it fell into ruin. The new church is said to resemble the old one in plan, and the windows are reminiscent of it too, but judging by the decline and criticism the previous church suffered, I would say a lot more care and attention was paid to the design and appearance of the new one.

Although the old church was still used in the 1880s, in a reflection of the criticisms of the building, relations between members of the congregation were turning ugly. In January 1884, a columnist in the *Cardiff Times* took issue with some of the customs and practices of the worshippers:

"Nothing is more indecorous than a scene in a place devoted to the worship of the Almighty … from Whitchurch there is a parish church in which seats are 'free and open'. A family in the congregation lays claim to a particular pew [and if anyone sits on it] they are incontinently hustled out by the claimants. [Some] add fuel to the fire by sometimes occupying the sitting for mere annoyance sake."

The article goes on to state that the previous Sunday, a "stalwart young fellow" did just that and a scuffle ensued. "What are the clergyman and churchwardens about in allowing such an unseemly exhibition?"

In March 1895, local discontent was brewing, advice to the Whitchurch Parish Council stating: "Decisive action was needed to confine the present burial ground to ratepayers and not allow the same to be used by outsiders from all parts of the globe."

By 1899, the old parish church was in ruin, and in February was reported as a run-down and vandalised monument of our past: "The church certainly makes a pretence of standing, but there is not a pane of glass left in either nave or chancel. The slates are falling from the roof, the roof timbers are trying their best to hold together, but they are fast rotting, and the walls, which support them, are crumbling away. A dozen or so of broken chairs are piled in the nave. The gallery is dangerous to tread upon, but, strange anomaly, the altar, with its altar cloth decayed and saturated by every shower of rain still stands behind the Communion rails, and on the pulpit desk still rests the damp and torn Prayer Book, inscribed 'Whitchurch Parish Church' ... Perhaps the chief features architecturally are the jambs of the porch entrance, which seem to date from the 15th century. They were probably brought from an earlier building. The earliest memorial slab, date from 1645 to 1697, but the majority are of the 18th Century. In the churchyard are the names of a great many well-known and wealthy families of the neighbourhood, and it seems a pity that something is not done to preserve the church and its surroundings, which would not be a difficult task."

The task of looking after the old parish church site has been taken on by the Friends of St Mary's Gardens, a wonderful group of dedicated and friendly local volunteers. Please do look them up, as they need all the help and support they can get.

St Mary's Church

In the late 19th Century, the state of the old parish church and the over-populated burial ground created many issues, to the point that T.W. Booker the elder, as churchwarden, was motivated to go to print to clarify some points that were causing discontent among parishioners. After two burials that were believed to be of non-parishioners, he made clear that he had no part in any decision making and had since determined that one was "virtually a parishioner and the other was so connected with the parish that all his relations lie there."

He was also determined to correct a wrong impression about "the acquirement of the land granted by the Ecclesiastical Commissioners for the site of a new church and churchyard." Reiterating the need for these, he stated that the Commissioners had concluded that a burial board would buy land and make a cemetery, at a cost to the ratepayers. It was the new Rev. Clarke, however, who worked tirelessly to obtain "a free gift of two acres of land from the Ecclesiastical Commissioners" and he appealed to the parishioners for their support.

On Wednesday 29 March 1882 at 3pm, Mrs T.W. Booker laid the foundation stone of the new St Mary's Church at Whitchurch, the old church lending its name to the new one. Funds had not been forthcoming in the manner hoped for and the opening ceremony had to be postponed on a few occasions. Were it not for the flags that streamed from the poles marking the boundary of the site, there would have been no signs of the work to be carried out upon it. It's interesting to note, however, that it was already being used as a burial ground before the construction of the building.

The new church was to have a "nave 58ft long by 33ft wide; a chancel of 37ft 6ins in length and a vestry and it was designed to seat 350 persons or more. The building which it is proposed to erect in the Gothic style of architecture will be surmounted by a square tower of 60ft in height and will have a very beautiful east window. Being in an excellent position, it will, we believe, be an ornamental acquisition to the village."

By June 1882, construction of the new church was well underway. The builders, Messrs Jones and Co of Gloucester, were making rapid and satisfactory progress. It was considered to be a "very handsome structure and decidedly a more fitting and becoming 'house of prayer' than the present miserable looking and dilapidated and unhealthy old church which is universally admitted as utterly devoid of any ecclesiastical or architectural propriety, the only church left in the district of this most deplorable description." So, no love lost on the old parish church opposite the Fox and Hounds in 1882, then.

In December 1883, a series of "Popular Musical Entertainments" was planned over the coming months to take place in the schoolroom, Whitchurch, for raising funds towards the purchase of an organ for the new church. It was not all plain sailing, though (nothing sacred is). In early March 1885, the post office in Whitchurch was robbed and a cash box was stolen. "The serious part of the matter was that most of the money belonged to the organ fund of the new church." £75 had been taken and £40 of it was for the organ. A few days later, an empty cash box was found under a hedge in a field along Merthyr Road, suggesting that the thieves must have been local.

In August 1887, news came through that the clock for the church tower, commissioned in commemoration of the golden jubilee of Queen Victoria, had finally been completed. It had three dials, two of 4ft 6in diameter and the other 4ft, with black backgrounds and gold letters. Tainsh Brothers, Cardiff, had carried out the work.

Much later, in April 1909, a "peal of bells [was] presented by Captain and Mrs Chappell of Greenhill." The bells were fixed into position and "were heard to advantage when the ringers attached to Llandaff Cathedral and St John's Church, Cardiff rang various changes". It must have been thirsty work, because "in the evening the ringers met at the Maltsters Arms Hotel and gave an interesting exhibition on the hand-bells."

St Mary's church hall

Another place of historical significance locally is connected to the vicarage and to St Mary's. It is the church hall in Church Road. The cutting below provides us with a little reminder of the value and the heritage of one of our community assets that is now desperately in need of investment and modernisation.

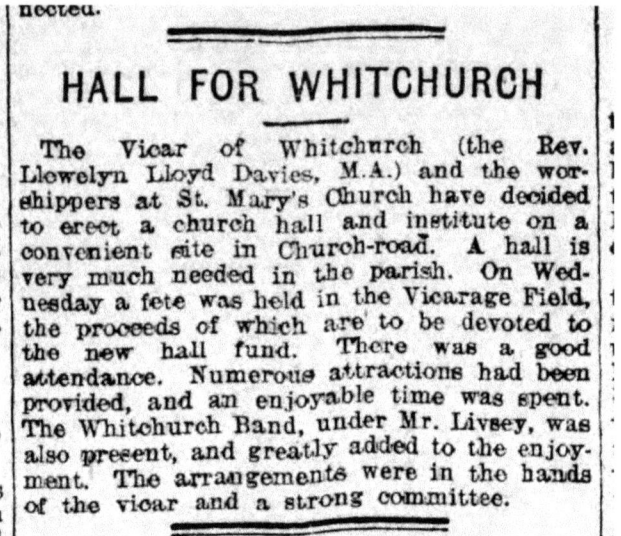

The Evening Express, 5 September 1907

The church hall would benefit from a thorough repair and renovation throughout. More could and should be made of this community asset – how sad it would be to see another place of local historical interest disappear.

Other Places of Worship

Ararat Church

This is a church with a history that dates back to 1824, so at the time of writing, it had just celebrated its 200-year anniversary. An offshoot from the Baptist church at Lisvane, originally a Welsh Baptist Chapel, for a period of its early life, it was also known as Wauntreoda Baptist Chapel, should you wish to do your own research. It has a long and detailed history that creates a defining image of Welsh Baptists – bible thumping, fire and brimstone, something some of us still remember from the 60s. It's not like that now, though.

Some books tell us it takes its name from the mound it was built on, others that it was built next to a mound, but neither sits well with me. Rather than burden you with my view on it here, if you are interested, my opinion can be found on the People's Collection Wales website (link at the end of this book). Alternatively, you can form your own opinion.

Here are some interesting snippets that you might not otherwise get to know about:

The first civil union took place on 4 January 1840, conducted by a Poor Law registrar, between Mr William Rees and Jane French. Presumably this was a marriage service, but I have included the wording as I found it written.

In July 1873, a treat was held at the chapel for the children of the Sunday School and the "College School, which belongs to the same chapel".

In its early days, Ararat Church was something of a cultural social hub, having its own choir and hosting many eisteddfodau as well as various lectures on weekday evenings. In March 1881, the Rev. J.G. Watts delivered a lecture entitled "The Red Indians". Native American was not the term used at that time.

The services were exclusively conducted in Welsh until 1878 when the church became bilingual. By 1882, this had caused a level of disharmony among worshippers and a division took place – a split that led to the building of a new English Baptist chapel on Penlline Road. A brief history is available online from the National Archives – Glamorgan Record Office / Archifdy Morgannwg.

In October 1893, "The Baptist Church at Wauntreoda made an application to Lord Tredegar for additional burial ground, the present ground being entirely taken up ... A large and most valuable plot of ground has been granted at a nominal rent." Lord Tredegar owned the area of the so-called common upon which the church was built. Other parts of the common had different owners, the major part owned by the Marquess of Bute.

Bethel Church

This church was formed in the year 1865. Services at that time were held in a small thatched cottage, occupied by Mr John Lewis, a shopkeeper. (I'm sure this was not THE John Lewis of the famous chain of shops, but how great would it be if you could make a connection?) Those who started the church were previously members of the Ararat congregation, the Welsh church at Wauntreoda.

A number of the members of Bethany Church, Cardiff, came to Whitchurch from time to time to assist in the formation of the new church, which soon found it necessary to move from the cottage to more commodious accommodation. The only building available for the purpose was a barn belonging to the Wauntreoda Farm, situated on the east side of the common.

Here, services were held for nearly two years, until a plot of ground was secured in a good position at the top of the main street in the village, at one end of which a small chapel was erected. This met the requirements of the church for some time. When another increase in accommodation became necessary in the year 1884, a building fund was started, Mr Richard Cory of Cardiff heading the list of donors with £50.

It was June 1894 when "The English Baptists of Whitchurch laid the memorial stones of a new building which will seat over 300", after having decided to build a new chapel. However, an event of entertainment under the name of Bethel English Baptist Chapel, Whitchurch was held in March 1880.

The opening service of the new chapel was in October 1894, but a sale of work (a handicraft sale) had taken place in the schoolroom of Bethel English Baptist Church in June 1894, the schoolroom being the original and oldest part at the rear of the church. The old schoolroom was still used as a Sunday school when I was a child in the 1960s, and was a convenient room for other gatherings. I hold a memory of it as a damp, dark, musky place, with old, creaky wooden floorboards and ancient dusty pews, ideal for learning map reading and compass work in preparation for the Duke of Edinburgh Awards with the Boys Brigade.

English speaking or not, in November 1897, the church held an eisteddfod. By then, Ararat had also converted to the English language.

The Tabernacle

The Tabernacle Chapel in Whitchurch is a grade II listed building. An old-fashioned classical design, it was originally a Calvinistic Methodist chapel built in 1866.

A plaque on its fascia provides the basic information, telling us the vestry to the rear and the adjacent house are both later builds. It is described as being listed as a "rare regional survival of a classical chapel with later 19th Century galleried chapel interior and for its group value with Bridge House opposite." The finials on the boundary walls of the adjacent house and on Bridge House over the road are similar.

Whitchurch Methodist Church (Wesleyan Chapel)

The church has a good website, which not only covers the building, but also summarises some general local history. It explains the link between Methodism and the Melingriffith works before worshippers bought a plot of land, the site of the present-day church.

The foundation stones for the new Wesleyan Chapel were laid in June 1894, "in the presence of a large attendance of the villagers and others". The opening of the new chapel was announced in January 1895.

"The new chapel which has been built near the crossroads, Whitchurch, by the Wesleyan Methodists was opened for divine service on Wednesday. The chapel is of the Gothic style of architecture and is an exceedingly pretty structure ... It's length being 80ft, and its width 40ft., with a schoolroom at the back. The total cost was £1,150, £779 of which has been cleared off."

A two-day bazaar was held at Ty'n y Parc, Whitchurch in July 1898, by kind permission of Mr J.H. Cory, to help extinguish the debt of the new Wesleyan Chapel at Whitchurch. Apparently, the Whitchurch Brass Band entertained the crowds on both days. We are left to wonder just how long it took to become debt free.

St Teilo's Roman Catholic Church

Classes for R.C. children in Whitchurch were first held in 1923 by a local school teacher in the home of her parents. As numbers increased, arrangements were made to use the schoolroom of Island Cottage (mentioned in the 'Buildings of Interest' chapter), before lessons moved to the old schoolroom near the Fox and Hounds pub.

Here, in 1924, the first mass was held since the Reformation. As numbers grew, the services moved to the pub's skittle alley. The church purchased the adjacent site and built a new church hall, which became known as the tin tabernacle. It was opened in April 1925.

Funds for the church we know today started to be collected from the early 1940s.

Sport

Sport in Whitchurch, throughout the generations, has played a huge part in the social lives of our people. However, you may be surprised at how much of our past sporting heritage has been lost. While there are still a good few successful traditional sports clubs in our community, it bears no comparison to what our predecessors once got up to.

Who, for example, knew that as early as 1906, Whitchurch had a baseball team? In May of that year, the Whitchurch team lost to Cathays United 42–31.

Let's now delve into the wonderful world of local sport. A link to more on Whitchurch sports clubs is provided at the end of this book.

Whitchurch Association football

You'll need to tread carefully if you wish to research two of the more traditional sports: rugby and football. Early on, rugby was commonly known as football, and what we now refer to as football was either soccer or Association football. Confusion can easily follow.

For simplicity, I will use the modern terminology, but be warned: the quotes are not so accommodating.

Cardiff City F.C. celebrated its 125-year anniversary in 2024, which included years when it was Riverside A.F.C., the name under which it was founded in 1899. One of the earliest football games in Whitchurch, if not the earliest, was in October 1901 against Cardiff Bank Clerks. The Whitchurch team was: (goalkeeper) W. Bailey; (backs) W. Evans and S. Price; (half backs) Campbell, Thomas and Rigg; (forwards) Evans, Greenslade, Churchill, Seaman and T. Shelper (captain).

Judging by various reports, it seems that by December 1901, Whitchurch had a second team. From the way newspapers reported things, there wasn't a formalised league system in place at that time; clubs arranged fixtures between themselves. By 1902, among the season's fixtures were matches against Cardiff Corinthians, but one standout fixture was in September 1902 when Whitchurch had a home match against... Riverside, the very same team that became Cardiff City.

The 125-year anniversary of football in Whitchurch will be in 2026.

Whitchurch rugby

Whitchurch Rugby Club has an extensive history dating back to 1885. In September of that year, a number of local people met "at The Three Elms Inn, Whitchurch and decided to start a [rugby] football club to be called Whitchurch Football Club". Even in the earliest days, village rivalry was intense; in December 1885, a match between Whitchurch and Taffs Well "came to an abrupt conclusion, owing to a very unpleasant incident", and it was decided that the result should be a draw. There was even a 2nd XV at that time, Whitchurch 2nds winning at home against Pentre. Perhaps this was a measure of local interest in the sport and the abundance of players who wanted to participate.

In a short time, the club became very successful with an impressive fixture list that included teams like the 2nd XVs of Cardiff, Newport and Swansea, as well as some of the larger towns in the region like Caerphilly, Barry, Aberdare and Pontypridd. It forged a strong link with Cardiff, frequently playing against the 1st XV in a season opener. One such match, in September 1895, saw a Cardiff XV team play against a Whitchurch XVIII.

There was more than just one rugby club in the village, too. Before 1890, there were Whitchurch Crescents, Whitchurch Juniors, Whitchurch Stars, the Y.M.C.A., Melingriffith Rovers and the Philog. By 1890, the Whitchurch Rugby Club was firmly established at the Fox and Hounds.

Some Whitchurch players turned professional and went north and a few became Welsh internationals. One of these was Johnny Williams who lived at Llwyncelyn just off Pantmawr Road. Johnny Williams died of his wounds at the Battle of Mametz Wood, France in July 1916.

Over the years, the fortunes of the club ebbed and flowed, like many others. Hardly surprising when all sports clubs of that era were to face the challenges of two world wars.

Whitchurch cricket

While Whitchurch Heath Cricket Club will soon (at the time of writing) celebrate its centenary year, cricket in the village can be traced back many years earlier.

Whitchurch Cricket Club wound up what was perhaps its inaugural season on 31 August 1878 with a match against Ely Cricket Club, winning by 28 runs. The match was played at Gwauntreoda (Whitchurch Common) and afterwards, both sides "sat down to an excellent repast, provided by the host and hostess, Mr. and Mrs. Morris, at The Three Elms Inn".

This, however, is not the earliest claim for cricket in the area. On Thursday 5 October 1865, a match was played between Ty Clyd and Machen, Ty Clyd winning by 36 runs. Ty Clyd is the old farm on Whitchurch Hospital, now the site and home pitch of Whitchurch Heath C.C.

By 1902, Whitchurch laid claim to four cricket teams: the Whitchurch 1st and 2nd XIs; Y.M.C.A.; and Hawthorne. The conditions of the playing facilities, however, weren't to everyone's liking. In May 1902, the local paper commented that the Y.M.C.A. should apply to the parish council for the use of the recreation ground because it "would be much better than playing on the common", a point that was made on more than one occasion due to the poor surface there.

When we were sure-footed children, lumps and bumps weren't an issue for us, but finding a flat, level surface for the wicket did challenge our entry-level surveying skills.

Amalgamation of clubs

In October 1892, plans were suggested for the Whitchurch cricket club and rugby clubs to amalgamate. "If the proposals now talked of can be brought about 'the loveliest village of the plain' will be able to boast of a good amateur athletic, cricket and football club." The plans were underway by September 1894, under the name Whitchurch Athletic Club. Club rules had been drawn up and the "objects of the club for football, cricket, lawn tennis, cycling, gymnastics &c., were established", but later there was a hitch regarding a field near and owned by the Fox and Hounds, now the site of Whitchurch Comprehensive School. A letting agreement with the landlord of the Fox and Hounds pub (Mr Allen) had increased from £50 to £100 (presumably this was / annum) and this was not considered acceptable. Negotiations followed for some time before an agreement was eventually reached.

Whitchurch hockey

Hockey in Whitchurch has a deep-rooted history that goes way back over 120 years. The current Whitchurch Hockey Club has an impressive record equal to any of our sports clubs.

In November 1903, *The Evening Express* published a short article that read: "Whitchurch Hockey Club – the first of its kind in the Whitchurch district has recently been formed ... a good field has been secured near Llandaff Station." This was on the polo ground – more on this later. Meetings were held in The Railway Inn and over the next few years, the club flourished.

In April 1906, a South Wales Scratch XI beat the Welsh team. Having been defeated in their international matches, the Welsh team, who had been criticised for the "mode adopted in the selection of the team", were challenged to a match against the Rest of South Wales, to be played "at the Whitchurch polo grounds in the presence of a fair attendance of devotees of the game". The Rest of South Wales team included D.T. John; R. Thomas; W. Shepherd; R. Buckley; T. Page; and W. Pallett, all from the Whitchurch club, with some of these also jointly representing Cardiff University. The score was 1–0.

Although records are rare, we know that Whitchurch must have had a ladies' team as early as 1906 when Ms A. Lewis (Whitchurch) represented Wales against Scotland as one of the backs. She had also played against Ireland earlier that year.

Many hockey internationals and representative games, male and female, were played on the Whitchurch polo ground, which is now a 1950s housing estate in the Ty Nant / Maes Glas area, a reminder of just how much our community has changed.

Athletics

In the late 1870s, an annual sports fete and gala was held in a field opposite the Maltsters Arms in the village of Whitchurch. In July 1879, a procession from the pub to the field was preceded by the Pride of the Valley Band, Whitchurch. However, some disappointment was expressed at "the number of people present as was expected from the attendance of previous years".

Apart from the shows, swings and roundabouts, "the greatest interest was centred on the footraces announced to take place between local amateurs. One side of the ground was utilised for a course and a very excellent one it made." Among the events were 100-yard, 150-yard and quarter-mile handicaps, and a "120-yard handicap was run for members of the club". The list of events was interesting mostly because there was prize money – for example, the 100-yard handicap: 1st prize £1 and 2nd 7s 6d.

In August 1883, a field belonging to Mr Wride of Village Farm held a sports meeting. Village Farm was where Domino's is now, the former site of our last proper Post Office. Although the weather was fine, the attendance was not as large as had been expected. A report described the venue as being in a field adjoining the Maltsters Arms, which gives us a better idea as to where it was.

In September 1892, a fete was held in Whitchurch, "owing to the successful initiation of a programme of athletic sports which are destined to become an annual gathering". The main objective was to "augment the funds of the village band". A track was prepared behind the Fox and Hounds and was considered to be "the best grass track in the neighbourhood … 200 entries were secured including the majority of the leading cracks of South Wales".

The events included a 120-yard boys' handicap (winning time 14.25 seconds); a 2-mile bicycle handicap (winning time 6 minutes 48 seconds); a 440-yard flat handicap (winning time 52 seconds); a 1-mile bicycle handicap (winning heat times around 3 minutes 20 seconds); and a 120-yard flat handicap (winning time 12.25 seconds).

"As a result of the recent sports at Whitchurch, a balance of £17 resulted [sic], which sum has been handed over to the Whitchurch Brass Band."

As touched on earlier, on 30 August 1894, the National Schoolroom hosted a well-attended meeting to amalgamate the cricket and rugby clubs and form an athletic club. The proposed rules were gone through and approved, but the field near the Fox and Hounds Inn hit a hitch, because of the letting terms of the land. To open the rugby season, Cardiff R.F.C., the champions that year, had agreed to play on the new ground on Wednesday 19 September.

In June 1895, "The Whitchurch Sports to be held on Saturday, give every promise of being eminently successful. The entries include most of the best runners in the district and with such excellent fare the attendance ought to be a record one."

The event left a bad taste in the mouth of one newspaper reporter over the cycle racing, however, due to the "effrontery and downright dishonesty of several prominent racing men ... if I had been the judge of a certain heat I should have promptly disqualified every rider." A 'swindle' was how it was described, with the winner accused of being aware of the swindle.

"Had it been an honest race he would have had about as much chance of winning as a pig has of flying." Perhaps a few side-bets influenced matters.

By July 1908, the Whitchurch Sports had moved to Birchgrove "under the auspices of the Birchgrove Rifle Club". A large programme of athletics events was completed – 120 yards; 440 yards and 1 mile – as well as events for juniors. The cycling included a half- and 1-mile handicap. Glamorgan County Police won a "handsome gold medal" in the tug of war with mainly men from Barry Docks, Central Station.

Bowls

In 2025, under the auspices of my old friend John Pearce (chairman) and the presidency of Bob Smith, Whitchurch Bowls Club celebrated its 100-year anniversary. It published a book to mark the occasion (*Whitchurch Bowling Club – Centenary Year 1924 – 2024*) and I was fortunate enough to be given one.

Bowls, however, was played in the village a lot earlier than people may think. In February 1903, a local newspaper published: "Whitchurch, lively though it is, is almost dull compared with the old times. William Thomas, a yeoman of the village was prosecuted for being absent from church and in 1720 several Whitchurch labourers were proceeded against for playing bowls on Sunday." Wicked times indeed!

The current bowls club is very welcoming. It has an excellent record and modern facilities, and a lot of hard work has been put in over the years to secure its place in our community.

Prize fighting

The pugilists among you are likely to be well aware of the bare-knuckle fighting that once, discreetly, took place in pub yards and back alleys, but in September 1898, a prize fight took place in secret between a "Gentleman and a Pro ... just outside the northern boundary of Cardiff". It was "fought with a determination not often seen in these encounters in this part of the country".

It was held in a disused barn and neither fighter was local, one being a "pug with far more than a local reputation and the other an amateur who had been successful in boxing competitions". It was so secret that less than half a dozen Cardiffians witnessed the fight, the remainder being strangers from the Midlands and London. The stakes were high, £50 a-side.

There was no police interference: "The exact location of the county constables was known to those who engineered the meeting place." The betting ruled 3:1 in favour of the pro, but the amateur won and apparently won well.

In March 1899, following a clampdown in other parts renowned to be "the scene of several 'merry mills' and the old rules", "Whitchurch has of late been the favourite battle ground. Possibly it was owing to the assizes which had drawn the county police to the borough that the old time battle ground was reverted to. It is years ago now since that there was a fight on the same spot as this morning. Then it was between Jack Welsh and Phil Reardon: but it was only of the 'short and sweet' order for almost as soon as the stakes were pitched, only a couple of short rounds had been fought, the police interfered."

Cycling

On a Thursday in June 1896, a meeting was held at The Plough Hotel, Whitchurch for the purpose of discussing the advisability of forming a cycle club for the parish.

The meeting minutes state: "The subject was taken up with much enthusiasm and it was decided to form a club to be called the Whitchurch Cycle Club." At the time, there were about 30 cyclists living in the parish and there was an expectation that the number could be "swelled by the admission of the fair sex, if they could be prevailed upon to give the movement their support". A meeting was then scheduled for the following Saturday to appoint a captain and establish the rules for the club.

Unfortunately, the cycling club did not last. One newspaper reporter, when commenting on regional sport in May 1903, said, "Years ago the Whitchurch Sports were most enjoyable. They ran the cycle events on a good grass track. A correspondent suggests their resuscitation." It does make you wonder what happened. Clubs disband for all sorts of reasons, but you would be inclined to think that a cycling club based here would be successful.

Tennis

The site of the polo field, which has been mentioned previously, also had a tennis ground. Neither are shown on the 1901 O.S. map, but they are on the one from 1922. The amalgamation of Whitchurch rugby and cricket clubs in 1894 formed an athletics club that listed lawn tennis as part of its offerings, and so that could well be the first date the sport was formally played in Whitchurch.

In September 1910, *The Rhondda Leader* newspaper published a brief article, which stated, "At a tennis tournament held recently at Whitchurch, two Llwynypia players, Messrs. R. Bowen and J. Haydn Jones, secured first and second places respectively out of forty competitors. Each was presented with a gold medal."

The present club was previously known as the Park Lawn Tennis Club and it had a very old wooden pavilion near its entrance (known by us locals as the Tardis, bigger inside than it was outside). This was part of the club's quaint character, all of which has now been replaced and modernised with all-weather courts and floodlighting. The club, like others, is a valuable part of our community.

Polo

The Glamorgan Country Club, formed in Cardiff in October 1900, eventually established itself at Whitchurch. "A suitable field has been obtained at Whitchurch and two sets for jumping have been erected, one for beginners, whilst suitable provision has been made for the military section. About fifty members have already enrolled."

By May 1903, after overcoming a number of obstacles, Glamorgan Country Club had become known as Cardiff Polo Club. "Among the prominent Glamorgan sportsmen who have joined the new Cardiff Polo Club—the first polo club, by the way, ever started in Wales are Lord Tredegar, The Mackintosh of Mackintosh, and Captain Rowland Walker [names to conjure with]. Captain Lionel Lindsay, a kinsman of Lord Tredegar, was acting as honorary secretary, and a seventeen acre field had been rented for play at Whitchurch."

It did not take long before there was a polo accident. This report appeared in the local newspaper: "Captain Forestier-Walker Injured at Whitchurch … In pulling up his horse sharply the animal slipped and fell upon the rider. Several members of the Whitchurch Ambulance Class who were present rendered assistance, but they could not ascertain if the captain had broken any bones ... Dr. Taylor's examined revealed that Captain Forestier-Walker had sustained concussion of the brain and other internal injuries. Messrs. Berwick. S. T. Griffiths, W. Compton-Chivers, and Police-sergeant Phillips were the members of the ambulance class who attended to the captain's injuries."

Given the social standing of some of these people, evidenced by the double-barrelled names which were very much reserved for the upper-classes in those days, it is easy to conclude that polo was a sport for those with a bit of leisure time at their disposal, although it's interesting to note that there was a distinctly military connection, strictly officer class. This niche appeal may well have led to polo's demise in later years.

By June 1904, it was the Cardiff and County Polo Club. Admission was free for members and 1 shilling for non-members. There was a members' enclosure where tea was served. Non-members with a voucher could pay 2s 6d to enter. Presumably the voucher was provided by a member, validating the good character of the non-member. Don't want all-sorts coming in.

In April 1905, a new pavilion was opened: "A very neat and pretty structure ... it contains two well appointed dressing rooms, besides a refreshment room." It is believed to be the same pavilion as that used by Park Lawn Tennis Club years later, right up to the 1960s/70s, having been moved from the polo field.

Before we leave Whitchurch polo ground, there was an interesting event in September 1911, which must have had people running from miles around just to witness it. From Weston-super-Mare, a Blackburn monoplane flew across the Bristol Channel to Cardiff and landed on the polo ground. The distance it covered was 16 miles and it took 16½ minutes. A few days later, it flew to Cardiff, circled the city and returned.

There are a good many of us who were born and raised on the estate that was built on that old polo ground (Maes Glas, Tynant, Erwlas). It wasn't unusual in the 1950s and 60s to find the odd horseshoe when gardens were being turned over.

Hunting

Granted this is no longer acceptable in many circles of society, but it was once a staple of sporting life for the privileged classes, and news records of hunts provide us with some detailed information of events that we would not otherwise be aware of.

One such record appeared in 1824: "Notice To Sportsmen, &c. – The old Annual Whitchurch Hunt Dinner will take place at the Fox and Hounds on Monday 27th September instant. The Hounds will be in the neighbourhood at ten in the morning and Dinner on the table at three precisely." The use of the pub for events of this type would undoubtedly have been the reason for its name.

You will, however, notice that the present pub has a nice, agreeable sign, depicting a fox harmoniously alongside a hound, having moved away from the traditional sign glorifying the hunt. Not really faithful to its origin, but *c'est la vie*.

Another notice appeared in May 1863, promoted by Mr J.P. Booker of Greenhill and Mr W.M. Lewis of the Heath. This time it was for otter hunting with hounds in Llanishen. I will spare you the gruesome detail, but a similar event took place a week later with the hunt claiming five large otters for the season.

The justification for this was that Llanishen brook was noted for its excellent trout, which was under threat by the otter population. This is a sign of both the times and the local environment, which gives us such abundant wildlife on our doorstep.

Other sports

Who would think that a foot race would cause a huge level of annoyance? Well, one did for a particular Whitchurch resident in June 1869.

This local man aired his views in the newspaper, and he didn't hold back: "The Forthcoming Foot Race At Whitchurch—Of all nuisances those immediately affecting life and limb are most to be guarded against, and there are few things more obstructive, and dangerous than races of all kinds along turnpike roads. The beastly exhibition of a fight is always conducted in a field or some by-place affecting none but the principals and those who delight in such scenes; but foot-races in public thoroughfares come like a mountain wave of the sea sweeping all before them endangering alike the safety of all travellers along the public roads, of which the abject beggar has as much right to avail himself as our beloved Queen herself; and above all other places in the hundred of Kibbor this contemplated outrage of public decency, of men running almost in a state of nudity, accompanied by the shouts and bellowing of artisans, on horseback, in vehicles and on foot is to take place on that mile of the Merthyr and Cardiff roads extending from the Holy Bush to the Maltsters Arms passing by the parsonage of Whitchurch, and close under the nose, as it were, of the chairman of the petty sessions of the district, a gentleman who has fairly trod in the footsteps of his father, by maintaining an unusual degree of order and general good conduct amongst his numerous dependants.

"It is rumoured that the race is made, and will be countenanced, by one bearing a name that shines chief among the manufacturers of Great Britain; but these *hebentes homines* should never be allowed to over-ride the law, notwithstanding that it is said matters have been made all right with the police. We have the inspector of police at Llandaff, sub-inspector of nuisances for Llandaff and Whitchurch, his chief being the energetic superintendent of police at Pontypridd and I ask, how can either of them, without blushing bring a poor carter who may be caught resting himself on the shaft of his vehicle, and have fined heavily, if they do not put a stop to a nuisance so fraught with mischief."

I'm not sure if you understand all that, but the writer seems to have been disproportionately offended by the prospect of men in running kit racing through the village.

Trotting matches were another sporting event that happened locally, the course generally being from Maindy to Whitchurch, a straight run of two miles. One of these events was held in October 1874, with the road for the whole distance lined by spectators on foot and in cabs. On this occasion, Mr Hopkins' horse Just In Time, ridden by Eli Hopkins, ran (trotted) against Mr Wiltshire's horse ridden by a professional from Gloucester. It was such serious stuff, the referee came from Charing Cross. Mr Hopkins' horse won easily.

In July 1890, there was an "Exciting Race at Whitchurch". It happened on Caerphilly Road. "The well-known trotting cob 'The Express' had been backed for £20 to trot a hundred yards faster than it could be run by E. Hughes, the noted sprinter living at Mountain Ash. 'The Express' was not to be ridden, but to be driven by a man mounted on another horse, the little quadruped being allowed to either gallop or trot ... The pedestrian won by a couple of inches."

Competition? Sport? What do you think?

Let's bring this chapter to a close with another question: how do you feel about a peg-leg race? Yes, it happened here. In June 1903, the papers were full of it: "Great Public Interest in Today's Event"; "By far the most comical walking race yet held in Cardiff"; "It was a competition for the wooden-legged fraternity". The course was from the old Rose and Crown near Kingsway, Cardiff (a popular traditional pub, sadly no longer there) to the fourth milestone at The Hollybush, Whitchurch, where a lunch awaited the competitors. Twenty-four took part and thousands lined the streets. Just for the record, the race winner was W. Popple (Cardiff).

Our sports clubs, or what is left of them, are at the core of our community and make a fantastic contribution to it. They are all very well organised and managed, and are well worth supporting and getting involved with, either as active participants or social members.

Give them your time. You'll make friends for life.

Societies

The various societies in the village were inextricably linked with the local pubs, their good intentions being to support people and families who had fallen on hard times. Some were formed from the workplace and some from the trades. You will now know of the Wauntreoda Show, later the Whitchurch Horticultural Show, which was known in its early days as the Melingriffith Floral and Horticultural Show, these being run by the societies of the same name.

In October 1856, The Maltsters Arms Inn Money Club met to celebrate its anniversary. It had 80–90 members.

The Treoda Lodge of the Independent Order of Odd Fellows met on its anniversary in July 1859 in its lodge room at the Maltsters Arms before the members held a procession to the Philog and to church, returning to the pub for a substantial dinner provided by their host William Evans, the landlord.

In September 1874, the Independent Order of Good Templars, belonging to the Hope of Whitchurch, celebrated its first anniversary. A procession formed, headed by the "Mellin-Griffith Templar" brass band, and paraded the neighbourhood.

In July 1885, the Ancient Order of Foresters, called Court Glan y Nant (No. 6884), celebrated its anniversary in the Masons Arms, Whitchurch. The members marched from the Masons to the new church for a service. Two of them, dressed as Robin Hood, headed the procession. Don't ask, perhaps no other fancy-dress costume was available. The Ancient Order did so again in 1886.

In August 1892, the members of the United Order of Oddfellows met at the Holly Bush to celebrate their anniversary.

In July 1898, the Penarth and Cardiff District of the Loyal Order of Ancient Shepherds held its half-yearly meeting at the Taff Vale Lodge, Maltsters Arms, Whitchurch.

The Whitchurch Friendly Societies' Council began holding its meetings at the Maltsters Arms in February 1900, and carried on for some years. In September 1901, it organised a demonstration in aid of the Cardiff Infirmary. The lodges taking part were Treoda (Oddfellows), Taff Vale (Shepherds), Pride of Glan y Nant (Foresters) and the branch of the Cardiff and County Annuitant Society. They raised £20 on their march, a sum which included £5 donated by the Melingriffith workmen. These workmen annually donated £15 to the infirmary, which increased to £20 that same year. They then decided to add another £20 to that, making a total of £45.

When Mr John Lewis died at age 81 years in September 1908, he was described as being "one of the oldest inhabitants of Whitchurch". We are left to wonder if he was the same John Lewis mentioned earlier in the section on Bethel Church. He was born at Heoldon and had worked at the Melingriffith for 50 years, having started in the mills before becoming chief accountant. He was active with the Wesleyan Methodists and held a proud record of having attended 69 anniversaries out of 71 in the old chapel at Melingriffith and the new chapel in Whitchurch. He acted as secretary of the old Melingriffith Friendly Society until it merged into the Shepherds' Society. He could remember the Whitchurch Flower Show being inaugurated in the bran-room of the works, before it went to Castell Coch, then Whitchurch Common and eventually Cardiff.

Apart from those mentioned, there were a few more societies at the Melingriffith Works, mainly due to the early 18th Century owners being Quakers, who are known for having a more benevolent approach to their own workers. Two of these were the Melingriffith Society and the Melingriffith Benefits Club.

Places of Note

Bonzo (Bondo?) Hill

The narrow sloping road mentioned in the 'Ty Mawr' section was known to locals as Bonzo Hill. Don't worry about the young cyclists of the 1960s who used to race down this hill at breakneck speeds – I was one of those cyclists, and I can assure you we used to have a spotter at the bottom to make sure no vehicles were coming when we free-wheeled down it on our bikes. There was not much chance of traffic in those days.

When the Glamorganshire Canal was there, Bonzo Hill led to a bridge that went over the canal. Known locally as Bonzo Bridge at the time, its official name was Melingriffith Bridge.

Sketch showing Bonzo Bridge as it passed over the Glamorganshire Canal to the fields beyond. Great House (Ty Mawr) and Bonzo Hill were on the left among the trees.

Something to ponder here is the name Bonzo. Depending on what part of Whitchurch or Llandaff North your family comes from, it is either Bonzo or Bonso Hill, and to others it is Bondo Hill. I could find no absolute evidence as to which is the official name, so you pays your money, you takes your choice!

The Glamorganshire Canal

Having just looked at Bonzo Bridge, we can't pass any further without talking about the canal itself. A quick history, and then we will look at the 'archaeology' we are left with.

Firstly, it is always referred to as the Glamorganshire Canal, and not the Glamorgan Canal or Glam Canal, which makes it sound as if it should have sparkling blue water and abundant supplies of freshwater fish. By the way, it is definitely not the feeder in Cardiff town centre. Two enterprises wore the Glamorganshire title with pride, one was the canal and the other was Glamorganshire County Cricket Club.

Way back in the mid-1980s, I had the privilege of acting as tour guide to two friends and work colleagues who were both active members of the I.W.A. – Inland Waterways Association. Both engineers, they had expert knowledge of canals, their history and operation. They planned to write their own book, but were thwarted by copyright issues with old photographs.

We walked its route, end to end, over a few weekends and a few pubs (one of these men was a member of CAMRA, the Campaign for Real Ale), from Cardiff Docks to the canal head at Merthyr. We retraced and tracked it, looking for any signs that linked us to the old canal. At that time, the overgrown and badly silted canal head in Merthyr still had the decomposed remains of two hulls of old wooden narrow boats.

The Glamorganshire Canal has been the subject of some good and useful books that are well worth reading. Completed in 1795, it stretched from Cardiff Docks to Merthyr, a distance of 25 miles, and was fully opened in 1798. Originally, it had 50 locks, as from Merthyr to Cardiff there was an elevation difference of 542 feet. Two other locks were added later at the Cardiff end.

You will probably well know that the canal ran through the eastern side of Hailey Park towards Ty Mawr Road. There it passed under the black bridge, which the T.V.R. now crosses. The old canal ran where the road does now, with just a footpath and towpath on the west side. A bit further along (northwards) is the location of Bonzo Bridge, between Cae Ty Mawr and Clos Ty Clyd.

As you go further along you come to Billy Williams' old place, Oak Cottage, which was once the lock keeper's home.

The sketch above gives an impression of how it might look today if the canal was still there (pure fantasy, of course). Oak Cottage is seen on the right. The lock is shown mid-centre, rising 10–15 feet to the upper level, the very reason the road now has an incline after the lock was filled in. This was Lock No. 44, Melingriffith Lock. Lock No. 1 was up in Merthyr.

Oak Cottage has a relic from its working days. A piece of open archaeology remains on the side wall to the rear of the property: an old cast-iron mooring post. When the cottage is cleared of hedging that grows alongside it, there are distinct markings of rope abrasion from its industrial past, worn into the post.

Just over to the west side of the road (left of the area shown in the sketch) is the old Melingriffith pump. This was located on an outlet feeder of the Melingriffith Tin Works because of legal disputes over water rights between it and the Glamorganshire Canal Company, of which there were many. It is said to have been designed and built by the eminent engineer John Rennie in 1807.

In principle, excess water flowing out of the Melingriffith Works along a feeder into the Taff drives a huge paddle wheel. As the wheel rotates, it drives two lever arms, one going up as the other comes down. The ends of the arms are connected to two pistons, each of which in turn is plunged into the water below. As each arm lifts, it pulls a volume of water up, which flows into a channel at the top that directs it a short distance into the canal alongside.

However, there is some uncertainty about the origin of the wheel. Engineer Watkin George designed the original pump in 1793, but it is unclear whether the Melingriffith pump is his or not. John Rennie's machines were known as fire engines and were used at a few places, following legal cases over water supplies between the different iron works and the Glamorganshire Canal Company.

The pump that stands there today is a replica, most of the old wooden parts having decomposed due to time and neglect. It was reconstructed during 1974–1985 by volunteers from the Oxford House Industrial Archaeology Society, Risca. Some of the original parts were on display at Risca museum. In 2011, it was refurbished, with an electric motor installed to provide rotation. Unfortunately, it has now fallen into disrepair once again, and flooding of the electrics has not helped too much.

The pump has an information board alongside it. It is supposedly the only one left in the world and is designated a scheduled monument. A model of it was built by a man named Roger John and can be seen on the Royal Commission on the Ancient and Historical Monuments of Wales website. Just alongside the pump are the rusting remains of an old bridge, placed there when the Melingriffith Works was demolished in order to build the housing estate that stands there now.

This bridge was located at the entrance to the works very close to the canal basin. It spanned the canal at that point to enable foot and wheeled traffic to cross.

There is an interesting feature of this rusting relic that is worth pointing out. With the canal passing under the bridge, the towrope from a horse-drawn canal boat or narrow boat would have had to pass over it to maintain motion of the boat, whether it was going upstream or downstream. The horse was unable to pass under the bridge, being as it was so low, and would have to go over and rejoin the boat on the other side. The rope would be unhitched from the horse and retied after the boat had floated under the bridge.

These were powerful horses, true beasts of burden if ever there were any, and they needed to be. Tonnage on the boats was high, the strain on horse and rope equally so. Evidence of this action and the rope tension forces involved can still be seen on the side rails of the bridge, shown in the photo below.

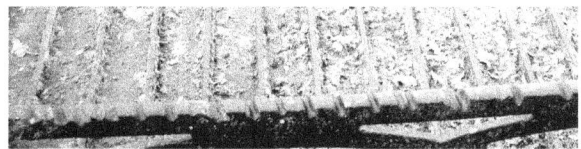

The side rails on both sides of the bridge show clear signs of rope abrasion over a long period. This abrasion indicates the direction in which the towrope was pulled and consequently the position of the bridge relative to the direction of travel.

Just a little further along northwards is the beginning of the nature reserve. Thankfully, this haven is a rare remnant of the old Glamorganshire Canal, a wonderful legacy of an industrial past, and the home to a vast array of wildlife.

The bridge in-line with the direction of the towpath that greets you as you enter is well used. A small weir under it allows a controlled amount of excess water to run off into the feeder on the west side. Many will know of the bridge, but may not have noticed that the two side rails are different. One is a straight horizontal rail and the other forms a curve, shown below.

In this photo, the Melingriffith feeder is on the right, the very end of the canal on the left. In its working life, the canal on the left-hand side of the bridge carried on straight ahead, gently curving to the right beyond this bridge and under the area that has since been fashioned into an accessible sloping walkway covering the route of the old canal.

For all those that don't know or have never considered it, back in the day, the bridge was part of the tow path, and the curved side rail allowed the tow rope to slide over it without obstruction as the narrow boat was pulled along by the horse.

An idyllic life?

As idyllic as canal life might seem, it was a ruthless world and you needed to be tough to survive. Rewards were not high, particularly in South Wales, where the iron and coal masters were not good payers, and transport and haulage was a cut-throat business. In glorious sunshine, there was probably nothing better than being out in the fresh air, floating along in the warmth, but British weather is seasonal and rarely complies.

I mentioned earlier my two work colleagues with a passion for the canals. Part of the field-work we did was to record an interview with an older Whitchurch man whose family, I believe named Bladen, was involved in the Glamorganshire Canal, on one of the working narrow boats. He worked it as a young lad with his father and grandfather. He had to get up early in the morning and attend to the horse in the stable, making sure it was fed, watered and harnessed. Meanwhile, his father and grandfather prepared breakfast and organised provisions for the day ahead. This happened in all weather, come rain, wind, snow, ice or shine.

One windy and frosty midwinter morning, wrapped up against the cold as best as he could, he left the house and trudged off to attend to the horse, but when he got there, he could not open the stable door. No matter how hard he pushed, it would not budge.

After a short struggle, he went back to the family house to get help. When he returned with his father and grandfather, sure enough, the door was unmovable. Eventually, they discovered that the horse, their only form of income, had died overnight and its huge body lay tightly against the door.

Such an event would have been catastrophic. Apart from losing the horse, the family also lost their ability to earn a living in a hand-to-mouth existence. Not only that, but they would have incurred a considerable cost to move and dispose of the horse's body.

Idyllic? I think not.

Whitchurch Library

On 11 April 1895, the newspapers reported that a poll had been taken in the village to decide whether the Free Libraries Act should be adopted or not. There were 73 who voted against it and 58 for, so the proposal was lost.

However, by the following month, the council was determined to establish a reading room in the parish, and the library committee, with the co-operation of several residents of the parish, acquired premises and made arrangements to open it. The total cost was £40, which included papers, periodicals, rent, services of a librarian and furniture.

The Melingriffith Reading Room Committee donated £20 on the understanding that men employed at the works would have free access to the rooms, and this offer was accepted. The new rooms were at the lower end of the village, in a house which the parish council rented for £34/year.

In September 1903, in a meeting of the Cardiff Asylums Committee, a letter from Whitchurch Parish Council was considered. It stated that the council had been granted the sum of £2,000 by Mr Andrew Carnegie, the famous Scottish-American philanthropist, to build a free library, asking for the committee's permission to erect such a building on a piece of land on the border of the site for the new asylum. The chairman said that when the committee had been given the land by Mrs Booker, there was a clause in the conveyance that no buildings should be erected there without the consent of the committee. Personally, he thought there would be no objection to a free library. This proposal was moved and seconded and the necessary permission granted.

It was not until December 1904 that the opening ceremony for the free library in Whitchurch was held. The members of the parish council assembled at the council school on Ty'n y Pwll Road where a procession formed. Leading the way were the members of the volunteer fire brigade in uniform and brass helmets, followed by the Whitchurch Brass Band. Next came the members of the parish council.

None of this, however, would have come about had it not been for plans to build Whitchurch Hospital (Cardiff

Asylum at the time). The land for the hospital was obtained by the purchase of the Velindre estate, owned by Mrs T.W. Booker.

Part of that land held a public right of way that led from Heol Don toward The Hollybush, where the old tithe barn was. The Whitchurch Parish Council fought tooth and nail to gain some form of recompense for the loss, and this eventually led to a triangular parcel of land, 4½ acres, being gained for recreational purposes at the crossroads. Later, a further planning concession permitted the construction of the library building on the site. It is this library that, in the early 1960s, gave us kids somewhere to go and hide behind the bookshelves. A place to hold back laughter and giggles, because they were not allowed in the strict discipline of library behaviour of old. I can still recall the feeling of bottling silent laughter, generated by the questionable authority of an intimidating librarian and the challenge not to get caught.

Whitchurch Hospital

The proposal to site a hospital in the village has been a bone of contention for a lot longer than you might think. Decisions made by the authorities often leave local people feeling impotent and abandoned. It is not new.

At the end of November 1897, the old schoolroom accommodated a meeting held by Whitchurch ratepayers to protest against the proposed location of an isolation hospital. Two sites had been mentioned, "both in the centre of a district which will probably eventually be thickly populated". A deputation was appointed to seek an interview with the Llandaff and Dinas Powys District Council, and in December 1897, two representatives of Whitchurch attended a meeting of the Council to protest against the proposals.

"The Chairman stated that a hospital must be put somewhere and it was [up to] the county council to say where they would like it fixed."

While this was going on, Cardiff Corporation eyed expansion. "[They] have now decided to apply for powers to take the whole of Penarth, part of the parish of Leckwith, the parish of Llandaff and parts of Whitchurch and Llanishen into the borough." One interesting commentary was "The parish of Whitchurch has an area of 3,269 acres and the population is 3,340. The area that it is proposed to incorporate amounts to only 10 acres."

In November 1899, "A special meeting of the Whitchurch Parish Council was held ... to consider the proposal of the Cardiff Corporation to erect a new asylum at Velindre." It was then decided to appoint a committee to get further details from the Cardiff Corporation, air concerns over the preservation of footpaths and ensure the interests of the locality were safeguarded.

Bring back the Parish Council, some might say.

It did not stop. In December 1902, there was huge controversy: "Whitchurch in Arms – Against Location of the Isolation Hospital – Project Said to Have Been Promoted Secretly. Information has just reached Whitchurch that the Llandaff and Dinas Powis [sic] District Council have virtually decided to erect an isolation hospital there and do away with the building already used for that purpose near Radyr ... Some time ago the ratepayers at a public meeting voted against a hospital being built in the parish and steps will be taken to pass a similar protest against the present movement." One site being eyed at the time was "a spot just opposite the Hollybush Hotel, Whitchurch".

The old hospital remains as much a part of our heritage now as at any other time since it was built. It is an iconic part of Whitchurch, but for how much longer? Who can tell?

It is deserving of a book in its own right. Many have benefited from having worked or been treated there, and from a community viewpoint, football, rugby, tennis, hockey and bowls have been played there. Being as Whitchurch does not have a leisure centre or football, cricket, or rugby pitches, and with the tennis club now under threat, you could argue that the hospital has been the centre of sporting life.

Let's now take a look at its early days, and before.

Negotiations

In August 1899, a meeting of the Cardiff Corporation Asylums Committee considered several sites for building a new hospital. These were Germonds Farm near Cowbridge; Windmill Farm (part of Llansannor Estate – £35/acre); a site at Peterston-super-Ely; a portion of the Velindre Estate (the property of Mrs Booker); and a 67-acre site in Llancarvan (£120/acre). It was agreed to inspect the Velindre site, providing there were 100 acres available there.

That month, the committee took more interest in the Velindre site, which Mrs Booker was prepared to sell (no price mentioned). "The property on the south-western side of the Cardiff Company's new railway consists of 115 acres. Because a great deal of levelling would be necessary the land on the north eastern side, although at a higher level was not considered suitable. The water conduit of the Cardiff Corporation and the Ystradyfodwg sewer are close to the suggested sites."

It was also stated that "there would be no difficulty in getting a siding from the Cardiff Railway to the asylum" if the site was chosen. One drawback was the comparative proximity of the Melingriffith Tin Works, probably because of air-borne emissions. It was at this time that the agent of Mrs Booker, Mr L.D. Nicholl, played an active part, offering plans and particulars for the site. Another concern was that a man named Mr Vyvyan Robinson held the lease of Velindre Hall, which was not due to run out until 6 years' time, and he would have to be compensated for disturbance.

In November 1899, "the Corporation of Cardiff decided to purchase the Velindre estate at Whitchurch and use the site for asylum purposes ... subject to the approval of the Charity Commissioners". In December 1899, Whitchurch Parish Council was not too impressed with a letter from the town clerk seeking the closure of two footpaths, something the members would not give their consent to. A David-and-Goliath scenario followed, forcing the two parties to arrange hasty meetings. By January 1900 the parish council still refused to give consent to the closure of the footpaths, but agreed to reconsider the whole case.

One of these footpaths was between The Hollybush and Ty Clyd. The parish council reported, "the path was used by a considerable number of workmen and if it were closed they would have to walk a mile further."

In February 1900, the parish council met to consider the asylum scheme. By then, consultation had taken place between all the bodies concerned, who agreed to allow the Holly Bush footpath to remain intact. That path is still there today, a legacy of the hospital's history, saved by caring and compassionate parish councillors and the needs of the Melingriffith workers. However, the other footpath between the Tithe Barn and Heol Don, quoted as being "from Tai Bach to Heol Don" (Tai Bach being either the name the barn was known by or someone's loo), was to be diverted by about 200 yards from the corner of the crossroads. The parish council members agreed to consider it, but only if they were entitled to compensation, and made a demand for 4 acres of land near the diverted footpath at the southeast corner.

In March 1900, the Corporation of Cardiff stated it was "willing to lease the corner piece of land near the Cross Roads (about four acres) in lieu of the parish consenting to a diversion of the Tithe Barn footpath".

In May 1900, the Asylum Committee approved "the conditions and instructions for architects in the competition for designs and plans for the new borough asylum on the Velindre site, Whitchurch". The competition was not limited to architects experienced in the erection of asylums.

A few days later, the Cardiff Asylums Committee held a special meeting, to consider the Whitchurch Parish Council's communication on restrictive covenants. At first, the parish council had wanted the ground for recreation purposes, and then desired to erect a fire station there, while the committee believed that an arrangement had already been agreed. Finally, the parish council was asking for a free hand regarding the land, as long as it did not build within fifty yards of the asylum boundary.

"Several members [of the committee] showed impatience at the action of the parish council and a resolution was unanimously passed declining to grant this latest demand."

A few weeks later, things remained unresolved. The committee stipulated that "no building should be put up without the consent of the corporation". The parish council declined this restriction and the committee threatened to abandon the site rather than give Whitchurch Parish Council a free hand, on the basis that it would "destroy the value of the site for asylum purposes".

As far as the hospital is concerned, the design parameters for architects' consideration (May 1900) were for the building to accommodate 1,250 patients, 800 at first and 450 added at a later period. Architects entered their designs into a competition that had a preliminary stage and a second stage, with a £100 payment to all the competitors except for the successful one in the second stage. A payment of 5% of the cost of the buildings would be awarded to the successful candidate as a commission.

In July 1900, the Cardiff Asylums Committee considered a request to provide for private patients, on the basis that "relatives of lunatics would be prepared to pay 30s to £2 for separate accommodation". This was deferred, with the suggestion that "Velindra [sic] House might be used for private patients".

By 15 September 1900, 40 architects from all over the country had responded. The date of entry had closed, 21 days' extension time having been added in July, and 51 sets of plans had been tendered. In the second stage, it was discovered that one of the assessors had previously employed one of the architects. This should not have been allowed, but the architect refused to withdraw unless he was paid 100 guineas (£105). It was agreed to debar him from the second stage and pay up. The assessor apparently had no idea this particular architect had entered the competition.

In November 1900, the sum of £71,000 had been awarded by the county council of Glamorgan, after Cardiff relinquished claim upon the county asylum, in order to relieve the county council of the financial investment involved and the responsibility for future treatment. Prior to this, the patients (described as 'lunatic patients') had been sent to the county asylum at Bridgend. The Velindre site, extending over 188 acres, was approved and an application was made to appropriate £38,000 for purchasing it.

The case for such a hospital was emphasised by a news article in December 1900, expressing alarm at Cardiff having to send patients not only to Bridgend, but to Carmarthen, Chester, Wells and even further. Not only that but the lack of accommodation for patients was becoming critical, with the newspaper reporting, "only two vacancies at Bridgend".

Hold-ups and setbacks

By February 1901, the plans of Messrs Oakley and Skinners of Bristol had been accepted, and they explained that a period of 18 months would elapse before work could start. As is always the case with these kinds of projects, minor alterations were made to the various plans as the details were submitted. In August 1901, a scullery was included for providing refreshments for visitors, while the borough electrical engineer was procured for advice on lighting, heating and ventilation. All this did not escape the scrutiny of the local press, who briefed the public with a "how-not-to-do-it" commentary.

In March 1901, the members of the old Whitchurch Parish Council vacated their seats, satisfied that they had accomplished their term of office: "The ratepayers had been made richer to the tune of several thousand pounds. One of the last duties was to sign a conveyance from the Booker family to the parishioners of a freehold piece of land at the cross roads."

By April 1901, things were heating up. The Bridgend asylum was close to full – 130 patients were boarded there at a cost of £30/week, much more than it would have cost if the new asylum was ready – and it was suggested that the corporation should erect temporary accommodation at Velindre and 20 patients should go to Carmarthen.

Patients were being sent from Cardiff to wherever there was a bed, at the rate of one a day. It was suggested that "harmless imbeciles" could be boarded in private houses in Cardiff, but it was pointed out that "non dangerous imbeciles" were dealt with by the guardians and that 30 and 40 were now in the workhouse.

In June 1901, pressure was building: "On 31st March 1904, the committee of the Glamorgan County Asylum will have the power of turning out all the lunatics belonging to Cardiff, being unable to find accommodation for them after that date."

In May 1902, the plans were passed after a few outstanding difficulties had been settled, and in June 1902, a sub-committee was formed to consider arrangements for providing temporary accommodation for patients if the new asylum were not ready in time.

In July 1902, concerns were raised over increasing costs for care and the rise of "lunacy", whether due to "consumption of alcohol or to the greater stress and strain of present day life". Over a period of 5 years, it had been necessary to "provide for 342 patients in 1897 and 618 by June 1902".

In August 1902, tenders had been received for the foundation work, the costs ranging from £16,000 to £26,000. The architect (Mr Oakley, of Oakley and Skinner) said that he had not expected the prices to be so low! The contract was awarded to the lowest tender, from D.W. Davies of Cardiff, with work to be completed within 8 months, under a penalty of £100 for every week over that time.

In September 1902, the Llandaff Rural District Council gave the news that "the surveyor mentioned that the contract for the foundations of the Cardiff Asylum at Whitchurch had been let and Rhubina stone was specified for the masonry". The report went on to mention the "great deal of heavy traffic upon the council's roads other than ordinary traffic". The decision was "Cardiff Corporation should be written to on the matter".

Many issues followed, worthy of a book in their own right, some of them ending up in arbitration. Anybody who has ever been involved with any type of engineering or building project will likely be familiar with this. One interesting feature was that in January 1903, an amended plan was submitted showing a "proposed embankment for a railway siding for the carriage of stores &c".

In February 1904: "The Cardiff Asylums Committee decided to make a present of the clock which was in use at Velindra [sic] House, Whitchurch, on the site of the new asylum there ... the clock will be erected at the tram terminus in Fairoak Road for the convenience of passengers to and from Roath Park."

By March 1904, the deadline for removing patients was looming: "Fortunately for Cardiff the Brighton Corporation were able to take 100 males and 110 females at their asylum at Hayward's Heath." Although there was progress on the Whitchurch Hospital, the stipulated finish time was doubtful. In some blocks, workers were engaged on the roof and tenders were invited for 2,000 yards of unclimbable fencing for The Hollybush footpath.

In February 1906, contracts for "the telephones, fire alarms, tell tales, bells &c., were awarded to J. B. Saunders, Cardiff at a cost of £1291 – 18s".

During construction, there were many incidents, some resulting in fatalities. One worker fell from scaffolding, and in November 1906, a bricklayer, who was erecting a boundary wall, pushed back some bushes that were in the way and got a thorn stuck in his left hand. His face began to swell and he was taken to the infirmary with muscular stiffness. He died later and tests were carried out on the thorn that was removed from his hand, which revealed that the deceased died from tetanus accelerated by pneumonia.

Throughout, cost management was uppermost in peoples' minds. One bone of contention was an architect's fee of £300 for the farm (eventually, Ty Clyd farm) when it was felt that the staff of the city engineer could have done the designs. It all had the desired effect: by March 1908, costs were trimmed to a limit of £2,000 or £2,500, leaving it to others not to exceed this estimate.

The hospital opens, but the problems continue

By December 1907, thoughts were turning toward agreeing on an opening date for the hospital. On 15 April 1908, the new Cardiff City Mental Hospital was formally opened by the chairman of the committee of visitors, with between 200 and 300 invited guests present. On Saturday 2 May 1908, news was given that the new Cardiff Mental Hospital would be receiving patients by the end of the following week.

> fidential.—Richards, 23, Malefant-street, Cardiff. e1331u28
>
> CITY Mental Hospital, Whitchurch, Cardiff.—Hall Boy wanted, not less than 14 years of age; able to drive quiet horse; wages £15 per annum, with board, lodging, washing, and uniform.—Apply, personally, to the Medical Superintendent, between the hours of 10 and 1. e5131

The Evening Express, 28 March 1908

The hospital was completed at a cost of £350,000 and the buildings occupied an area of 4½ acres to accommodate 750 patients. In February 1909, a £2,174 tender for the erection of the farm buildings was accepted.

We covered the Whitchurch Pigs earlier, and pigs became a major issue in the design and construction of the old hospital. A lot was made about the scale of expenditure at the planning stage, with many expressing dissatisfaction at the corporation being "extremely extravagant in their estimate of what a lunatic asylum should be like" and complaining of "expenditure with an almost utter disregard for economy". Some of this expenditure, not least of all for the hospital plans on the construction of the farm and outbuildings that were estimated to cost £4,000, with £1,000 going towards the piggeries, invited universal ridicule. Even when this figure was later cut back, "The swine of the Whitchurch Palace will probably have to put up with something only superior to the stys [sic] of other districts."

All this relates to the long, drawn-out nature of the entire process and the scrutiny it came under. The farm was a controversial requirement, ostensibly for patient rehabilitation.

One newspaper, in October 1907, printed a cartoon of a lavish semi-detached residence with ornate Gothic arch, bay windows and numerous pigs lounging about at leisure. Such was the fractious nature of local feeling that when Cathays Park in Cardiff was being fashioned at the same time, one newspaper reported that visitors would have "their sense of artistry offended by the sight of three or four ugly pedestals surrounded by obelisks erected outside the City Hall. They look suspiciously like tomb stones for the Whitchurch pigs."

A dairy farmer from Abertawe (Swansea) was appointed from over 100 applicants as farm foreman. He was paid £2/week with house, water and light free.

Another issue concerning burying the dead cropped up in October 1907. As undignified as it may seem, it came down to cost. "The Whitchurch cemetery [is] charging four times the price that the guardians of the Cardiff workhouse were able to bury for." The suggestion was that "some of the asylum land behind the chapel be reserved as a private burial ground for the asylum". This, however, was rejected, the land being required for farm purposes and for supporting inmates.

"The land available for asylum purposes was too valuable, with all respect to the dead." The question of cremation as an alternative ended with the matter being deferred.

The tower

The hospital water tower is a monument of Whitchurch identity: tall, proud and defiant, an easily recognisable landmark for any wayfarer. It rises to a height of 150 feet and contains high-level cold water storage tanks for the hospital's engineering systems.

Have you ever noticed, though, that there is a large circle on three sides of the tower?

On 19 July 1906, *The Evening Express* provided an update on a meeting of the Cardiff Asylums Committee. This meeting decided that plans for a three-faced clock on the tower, costing £400, would not now proceed and the town clerk was instructed to "return, unopened, the tenders sent in for the work ... such a clock would be of no value except to the people of Whitchurch."

This could have been our Big Ben.

What would we have called it?

Big Ifor? Ifor Mawr, perhaps?

Tragedy

It goes without saying, such is life, that the village has had its fair share of tragic incidents through the ages.

At the end of November 1877, a well-known man in the neighbourhood, a mason about 60 years of age, was found drowned on a Sunday morning in the brook near the Fox and Hounds. It was supposed that he'd missed the small bridge during a flood on the Saturday night and slipped into the raging waters.

You will have read about Whitchurch pigs earlier, but here is one relating to a pig owner. In February 1885, on a Tuesday afternoon, Richard Neagle, living near "the Holly Bush [sic], Whitchurch", met with a very painful and untimely death. Neagle and his wife had been to Cardiff in the morning to buy some food for a number of pigs they were fattening. A cask about three feet high was kept near the pigsty in the garden for holding the pigs' food. The deceased was in the act of tipping a sack of grain into the cask when he fell in head first, and could not regain his footing.

"In this position, he was found later on, by a man named Evans, quite dead. Neagle leaves a widow and several children, and much sympathy is felt for the family."

Another pig-related incident happened in May 1896. The coroner held an inquest at "the Holly Bush Inn [sic], Whitchurch", into the death of Agnes Augusta Griffiths. The little daughter of Mr Griffiths of Holly Bush Cottage, Agnes was found dead in a tub of pigwash. The jury brought in a verdict of accidental death.

How unfortunate was Richard Lewis, a 21-year-old from Tongwynlais? Talk about being in the wrong place at the wrong time.

In November 1886, he was walking along the road in Tongwynlais, when "a bull that was being driven by a man to the slaughterhouse made a most determined attack upon him. The ferocious animal tossed the poor fellow over its head and then butted him so severely in the stomach that he died from the effects of the injuries he sustained."

In August 1895, during building operations in the centre of Whitchurch village, "...a number of men were employed, erecting shops. A young man named Harry Pike was engaged in excavating for draining purposes, when by some means the earthwork gave way and the poor fellow was buried. He was extracted as quickly as possible and Dr Arthur was sent for but death ensued."

Even before the days of motorised vehicles, some unfortunate people, including children, lost their lives in road accidents. How difficult could it have been to avoid the slow-moving vehicles of the day, even when motorcars were starting to appear on the roads? In February 1907, a 78-year-old man, a gardener, was knocked down and killed by a bus on Whitchurch Common. The driver said that he "did not see him until he stepped suddenly off the pathway and he was unable to pull up within less than four or five yards".

Farming life brought its own dangers. In October 1909, Mr David Davies of Glan y Nant Farm died after inadvertently shooting himself. He "went out early into one [of] his fields near the Melingriffith works for the purpose of shooting rabbits and while he was mounting a gate, the gun went off and a charge lodged in his side." His friend, who was with him, summoned assistance from the works, and a policeman and others rushed to the scene, but he died as they were attending to his wound.

In June 1910, two motorcyclists were returning home to Newport from a motor-hill climbing competition on the Whitchurch-Caerphilly Road. It was 5.45pm, and as one took the more direct road (Rhubina) into Whitchurch, the other went over the Caerphilly Road.

"At the crossroads at Birchgrove, where several accidents have previously occurred, the motorists [motorcyclists] went around the corner so swiftly that a collision was inevitable." One of the motorcyclists was killed, their machine completely wrecked.

What are the chances of the two motorcyclists arriving at precisely the same point at the same time?

Public Services

The post

Something that we once took for granted was a twice-daily 1st and 2nd class postal delivery service from the Royal Mail – their old mantra being "The post must get through." These days you are lucky to get your letters at all, a bonus if they are delivered to the correct address. We have regressed and we can now identify with this report from August 1882:

"The inhabitants of the Heath, a hamlet contiguous to the village of Whitchurch, are put to considerable inconvenience by having no postal, [sic] delivery. At present the letters are left by the Caerphilly postman at the Birch Grove Inn, and by the Whitchurch, [sic] pit-man at the Philog, and unless they are sent on to the parties whom they are intended for, they would not get them for days afterwards.

"Overtures have been made to Mr Webber, postmaster, Cardiff, accompanied by a memorial signed by a large number of inhabitants, to establish a delivery. The gentlemen who are moving in the matter have also pointed out to Mr Webber the desirability of erecting a letter-box at the Philog, alongside the Merthyr road, so that the postman who travels between Cardiff and Taff's Well may clear the box on his way to Cardiff. It is to be hoped Mr Webber will see his way to establish a delivery, and thereby confer a boon on the inhabitants."

It took a few years for things to improve, but not before people were required to follow the how-it-was custom and practice of collecting their own mail from the local post office. Perhaps this will come back, becoming a how-it-is practice.

Things changed in 1890, as the cutting below from *The Western Mail*, dated 8 August of that year, shows:

POST-OFFICE NOTICE.

A new letter-box has been erected near the Probate Court, Llandaff, and will be cleared four times daily on week days, viz., at 8.30 a.m., 3.20 p.m., 6.30 p.m., and 7.30 p.m., and on Sundays at 6.0 p.m.

On and from Monday next, the 11th inst., free postal delivery will be extended to Rhubina, Sea View, Brunant Farm, Wenallt, Graig, Ty'nycoed, and Gross Road Farms, Whitchurch.

The North mail correspondence now delivered to callers only at the Whitchurch Post-office will be delivered free from house to house in the village.

A new mail will be despatched from Cardiff to Whitchurch, and letters posted at the head Post-office, St. Mary-street, up to 12.30 p.m., and at the branch Post-office, Bute Docks, up to 12.15 p.m. will be forwarded in it, and be delivered in Whitchurch the same afternoon.

An additional mail will be forwarded from Whitchurch at 11.25 a.m., and the correspondence will fall into the mid-day delivery in Cardiff and into mid-day despatches to London, &c. An additional collection will be made from the Philog Wall-box at nine a.m. and Holly Bush Wall-box at 9.30 a.m., and be included in the new despatch from Whitchurch to Cardiff at 11.25 a.m.

How far have we gone in 130 years?

Gas, electricity and water

One thing we do still take for granted is that we flick a switch and on come the lights, or we open a tap and clean water comes out, then we pay for what we use. However, it wasn't always like that.

On 7 November 1885, a public notice was issued by the Llandaff Highway Board to announce that the road leading from The Hollybush to Rhubina and the Derry, in the parish of Whitchurch, would be closed during the laying of the Corporation mains, an early sign of a mains supply.

In September 1890 in Whitchurch, "Considerable difficulty is experienced in this neighbourhood in obtaining water just now, the usual sources upon which the inhabitants are dependent having for several days past been entirely dry. Work is suspended in some places and the public suffer much inconvenience by having to go long distances to obtain the smallest quantity." At the time, "the village pump was either dry, or out of repair" and local people were afraid of fever as they had to resort to "brook water, which has been well used by ducks and butchers".

At a meeting of the Cardiff Waterworks Committee, April 1892, "it was resolved to instruct the waterworks engineer to lay the main for the supply of water to Llandaff and Whitchurch and to engage men for that purpose forthwith."

Back in the day, the supply of gas was an issue as well. Whitchurch was expanding at pace. In September 1894, a meeting was held at the schoolroom to consider asking the Cardiff Gas Company to extend its mains to Whitchurch with a view to lighting the village. It was deferred until the parish councils were elected.

"A proposition to ask the company to extend their mains for the purpose of private lighting was defeated as it was felt that the company had so long deferred this matter that it now resolved itself into the question of the best terms." Committees! What would we do without them?

By April 1899, the need for lighting in Whitchurch was still far from being resolved: "[it would be] desirable if an arrangement could be made by which the parish of Whitchurch, or at least, a portion of it could be lighted by gas or some other illuminant." At this time, a man called Sam Allen came to the English Baptist Chapel to demonstrate his 40-light acetylene gas generator. The generator was placed at one end of the chapel and ¼-inch diameter pipes were placed around the church. About 3 lb of carbide was used during the evening, apparently costing 3d, and "the chapel was exceedingly well lighted with the ten jets."

A couple of years later, in October 1901, a monthly meeting of the Whitchurch Parish Council was held at the schoolroom to consider a report on the lighting of the parish and what progress had been made. Two lamps had been erected, one near the Post Office and the other at the Philog, and although the light was good, the council was of the opinion that better results could be obtained. The members were interested in lighting the darkest parts in the parish. An order had been given to Mr Evans, of the Eagle Foundry, Llandaff, for the supply of lamp posts, costing £2 9s 9d each.

It was mentioned that the Cardiff Gas Company was now in a position "to extend their main to the top of Church-road, so that private consumers in that part of the parish could obtain that illuminant, if they thought desirable". The acetylene system, when complete, would cost the ratepayers about half the price of ordinary gas.

Lighting and gas were still issues in September 1903, when the Whitchurch Parish Council held a special meeting at the Glanynant School to appoint a representative to act on the county education committee and take steps for lighting the parish during the following winter. A deputation was appointed to enquire of the Cardiff Gas Company its price for a supply of gas for street lighting.

The plan stated if the "terms are considered reasonable, the council will then use coal gas instead of acetylene as in previous years. It was reported that it was probable that electric light would be available for the winter of 1904."

In April 1904, The South Wales Electrical Power Company (Limited) was granted permission to lay cables to the Melingriffith Works, Whitchurch, and the Phoenix Brickworks at the Heath. The Whitchurch Parish Council chose to write to the district council to enquire what steps, if any, would be taken to light Whitchurch by electricity. Some years prior, the parish council had formulated a scheme to light the parish by electricity, but at the last moment, the Local Government Board stepped in and stated that a parish council could not generate the illuminant. The parish council then gave all the assistance it could to the district council to get its Provisional Order for providing street lighting. With this arrangement in view, the parish council members believed the village was entitled to consideration if the South Wales Company's cables were laid through the district.

By September 1904, the parish council remained frustrated after receiving a report from the deputation that had approached the district council: "It was decided to allow the matter to remain in abeyance for the present. The council confirmed a report of the lighting committee to erect eight extra gas lamps. The report also stated that the gas mains would probably be extended at an early date to the Heath district."

It dragged on for some time. In November 1910, Whitchurch Parish Council wrote to Llandaff District Council asking that two or three of the principal roads be lit by electricity. The parish council clerk said the Electric Lighting Committee merely wanted the authority of the district council to comply with this request, which was granted.

"It was resolved that the applications for the extension of the cable in Kelston and Wingfield-roads be deferred until the precise demand was ascertained."

By January 1913, the district council had an eye on costs. In front of a small committee, its clerk stated that the cost upon the collective parishes in the rural area of the electricity scheme at Whitchurch the previous year amounted to £438. It is worth pointing out here that the district councillors considered this to be a bit of a shame and bemoaned the ongoing cost of it, one stating that he opposed it to begin with, mainly due to the belief that there would be "profits that the concern was going to make". The matter was allowed to drop.

It is clear that the economics of supplying services to the community was closely controlled, even to the point that there was some resentment at the prospect of the utility companies making a profit from it.

Sewerage

On the subject of utilities, we can't pass by without a thought for sewerage. In another age, there was none. Today, apart from obvious hygiene benefits (obvious to us anyhow), we are more and more conscious of environmental issues, so good sewer systems are essential in our modern world.

However, it was only in October 1894 that the Whitchurch sewerage scheme was completed by the Cardiff Rural Sanitary Authority at a total cost of £4,860. It extended over an area of about 2,000 acres and had a length of about eight miles of stoneware pipes, varying in size from 6 inches to 15 inches in diameter, emptying into the trunk sewer of the Ystradyfodwg and Pontypridd Joint Committee system, which extended from the Rhondda to the Bristol Channel. The scheme was divided into five contracts and included automatic flushing tanks supplied by water from the corporation mains. The gradients were so regulated as to make the whole network of sewers self-cleansing, and the manholes and lamp-holes were arranged in order that any stoppages or obstructions could easily be found and removed.

The scheme was designed and carried out by Mr William Fraser A.M.I.C.E., the engineer and surveyor of the Cardiff Rural Sanitary Authority. Gauges were fixed near each connection with the trunk sewer to measure the quantity of sewage passing from the sewers of the authority. Each section was disconnected by syphons fixed near the trunk sewer to prevent foul gas passing through the system.

Strange to think that these old sewerage systems remain a controversial issue to this day.

Royal Visit

Whitchurch has had its fair share of noble residents over the years: the great and the good – the crachach or uchelwyr, depending on which side of the fence you sit on. However, none was so illustrious as a visitor in the early 20th Century.

In July 1907, King Edward VII made his way to South Wales. Part of his itinerary was a visit to Caerphilly Castle, travelling from Cardiff by road, and the route took his entourage through Whitchurch and Tongwynlais.

The parish council prepared for this by erecting three arches, one near the library, one near the Maltsters Arms and the other on the Philog. Elaborate decorations were also erected across the road near The Plough Hotel and residents on the main road from the top end of Park Road to the Philog were asked to put up private decorations. The council also decided to present each child on the register of the four schools in the parish with a medal in commemoration of the Royal visit.

Where are those medals now?

Pubs

Pubs and pub signs are an interesting part of our history and heritage. In many cases, the pub name has a meaningful connection to its past. The signs themselves are more than just an advertising emblem: some have unique designs, with many considered works of art.

Sadly, the traditional pub signs that once graced our village are long gone. All of them had signs displayed on a traditional sturdy oak pillar, positioned proudly on the edge of the pub's property, now replaced by apologetic gestures as a faint nod to their heritage.

Brewing beer centuries ago was commonplace, as drinking-water supplies could not be trusted and the brewing process was a means of removing impurities and other nasties for a far safer way of quenching the thirst. One of the centres for home brewing was the local blacksmith, a strenuous trade demanding a constant supply of fluid replacement. It is easy to see how a little sideline would be created, the blacksmith selling off excess beer to customers who had less capability or desire to brew their own, or even making extra for just that reason.

It was also common for beer and alehouses to display some kind of emblem linked to their trade or the community they wished to attract. Another historic connection to their origin, this was how pub signs came about. In some cases, beers and ales were brewed and sold on site, but the pub never actually had a name, leaving no traceable record. That could possibly have happened here in a few of our older pubs, before they adopted the names we know them by now.

In 1873, the district licensing authority oversaw eight parishes: Llandaff; Llanedarne; Llanishen; Whitchurch; Radyr; Caerau; Roath; and Lisvane (the outlying districts of Cardiff). The number of public houses was 68 and there were 30 beer houses. The total population of the district, according to the census of 1871, was 20,209.

Without exception, every pub in the district fell foul of the drinking laws of the day, violation of Sunday drinking and permitted hours being the main charge. Throughout the entire region, over the 12 months from 1908 to 1909, "174 persons had been proceeded against for various offences under the Licensing Act and all but 13 had been convicted".

The Plough

In the 1840 tithe map, the land the pub stands on is identified as a meadow. But, the pub itself almost did not happen. In September 1858, Reuben Lewis of The Plough, Whitchurch, made an application to the bench for a spirits licence, but it was refused, another public house in that locality being considered surplus to requirements.

Reuben Lewis was a blacksmith with a workshop just behind the pub we have now. He built his business around agricultural equipment – little doubt he would have had a farming background. Such was his expertise that he fashioned a horse-drawn plough in a way that made it more efficient to pull, which would have enabled more acreage to be worked over a given time. His plough set the standards for others to follow, winning competitions, providing a draw that others were measured against.

It was commonplace back in the day for blacksmiths and other traders and grafters (eg farm and land workers) to brew their own beverages, whether that be beer, ale, cider or some other concoction. In fact, it was essential for hydration. Natural water sources were considered unreliable, exposing the drinker to all sorts of contamination from their surroundings, with the potential for the nasty diseases and, in extreme cases, death that plagued larger towns and cities. The brewing process was believed to be more reliable and provide a more nutritious drink.

It is not difficult to see how excess supplies could be sold off to people who did not have the capacity to produce their own alcoholic drinks, and this would have been a useful opportunity for tradespeople to earn a bit extra. This is how many pubs and breweries were established, and there is little doubt that this was the case here.

The fame of Reuben Lewis's plough spread everywhere and he was able to expand and develop both his workshop and his beer house. In all probability, as was customary, he had a plough positioned on his forecourt, as a display to passers-by that his establishment was an inviting place for anyone involved with the agricultural industry.

Make no mistake, he was no impoverished metal basher forging horseshoes. He had manufacturing rights for the Ball's Criterion plough, a device that the original inventor won prizes for at the Great Exhibition of 1851, and he adapted it to make it more efficient. He manufactured a wide range of agricultural equipment on the site of his forge, and at one time, he expanded his workshop to include a casting capability and increased the steam power, presumably for power forging.

Unfortunately, it did not last and he later faced bankruptcy. He'd invested a lot into the development of his agricultural business capability, but this was at a time of mechanisation and a move towards factory farming methods. Manual labour and basic tooling began to decline, and valuable local farmland was being eyed up by planners and developers. Today, you would never know his smithy was ever there, but his legacy remains with us.

The Fox and Hounds

It is difficult to date this pub. It was clearly one of the earliest in the village, particularly so because it is located in the most ancient area, and it is reasonable to assume that selling and consuming beer or ale would have been a basic requirement back then.

It was definitely there in 1824, as in September of that year, the Old Annual Whitchurch Hunt Dinner took place there. It is also reasonable to assume that it took its name from the hunt following that used it as a base.

In December 1877, the then landlord John Jones was charged with permitting gambling in his public house, named in the local papers as the Fox and Hounds, Whitchurch. A huge, dreadful and addictive crime, you might think...

Two police sergeants had visited the pub and seen a box of dominoes and some chalk marks on the table. Around it were sitting seven men. As a result, two constables were sent to the pub in plain clothes. Later, in the witness box, they said that beer had been played for in their presence. The defendant, John Jones, was fined 20s (£1), including costs.

The moral of the tale? Look out for undercover agents in the corner of your favourite pub.

The Hollybush (Llwyncelyn)

Another old pub, this was certainly here in 1838 when the landlord was listed as Mr J. Jones. In its early days it was outside the village, quietly located in the countryside on the old turnpike road on the corner of the junction with Rhubina Road, now better known as Pantmawr Road. Surrounded by hedgerows and farms, it was a convenient location on the coaching route to the villages and towns beyond.

By the 1840s the licensee was William Lewis, the role seemingly shared with a George Lewis. Both were active participants and organisers of the Whitchurch Horticultural Show. We will talk later about the abundance of people called Lewis running pubs back in the 1800s.

In October 1858, the pub was one of the lots put up for sale by auction. It was described at that time as, "All that old established and conveniently situated road side inn". An indication, perhaps, of its antiquity.

Interestingly, William Lewis was still there in 1871, but in 1864, landlord Samuel Lewis – little doubt it must have been a family enterprise – was summoned for keeping his public house open on Sunday. He was fined 5s + costs, and our William was charged with the same offence in 1871 and fined £1 + costs.

In the 1890s, The Hollybush was a meeting-point for the Ystrad Hunt, giving us a flavour of the rural activities that went on here and just what many of our pubs were used for.

The Maltsters

This pub is probably older than you might think. In June 1853, Miss Hannah Evans succeeded to the business once owned by her aunt, so clearly the pub predates that year. Her house-warming dinner in July 1853 was attended by her numerous friends and was apparently a very influential gathering under a marquee on the site, so there must have been plenty of open space around the building at that time.

In the 19th Century, the Maltsters was a venue favoured by many groups from local industry. In June 1860, the agents and foremen of the Pentyrch Iron Works held a dinner there in honour of the Marquess of Bute, following his death. Through the 1880s and 90s, it was used by the Oddfellows Loyal Treoda Lodge. The Melingriffith workers' groups also met there.

In July 1864, it was put up for sale by auction as a leasehold property, together with its malt-house, adjoining eight cottages and "the piece of building ground adjacent thereto on the east side of the main road", a description that gives us some idea of the full extent of the linked enclosure. That same lot (with a few small changes) came up again for auction in May 1897.

Clearly, the mention of the malt-house – and the maltster or maltsters that worked there – is the link to the origin of the pub's name.

The Masons Arms

Of our traditional old pubs, this was one of the later additions, possibly a farm dwelling in its early life. However, it must have been a pub by the late 1800s, as it was the meeting place for the Ancient Order of Foresters – Court Glan y Nant during the 1880s.

One of the earliest records of the pub comes from 1871, when the landlord, James Thomas, was summoned for permitting gaming. His offence? "Allowing certain persons to play 'nine pins' for beer in his house." He was let off, but had to pay costs. The date might come as a surprise – did you know that skittles was played in this area all those years ago?

In December 1898, a large number of publicans in the area applied to the magistrates' court for extensions to opening hours for Christmas. Jacob Thomas of the Masons Arms, Whitchurch, asked for an extension from 10pm to 4am on 28 December, because "A cycling club was going to have a cold lunch and dance on that date".

At the hearing, the clerk responded, "I should think it would be cold by then", which caused some laughter.

The magistrate then commented, "They ought to be in bed by that hour surely. Why can't they commence the feast before 10?"

"Because they cannot arrive earlier," was the reply. An extension was granted until 2am.

The Masons Arms is a popular pub name, originating from a local craftsmen's guild. Whether or not this trade was the original use of this particular establishment is difficult to say.

The Royal Oak

The Royal Oak is another of our younger pubs, but it still has some age to it. What is certain is that its mock Tudor facade is more recent, dating from the early 1960s.

News stories concerning the pub start from the mid-1800s. In April 1867, landlord George Roberts was charged with permitting drunkenness and was fined 40s + costs or, in the event of default, one month's imprisonment. "The accused who had been before the magistrate before was severely cautioned."

Our George clearly didn't learn. In February 1868, he was charged again, and faced a further charge in October 1876, this time for keeping his public house open for the sale of liquor during prohibited hours. Most of these types of offences were for Sunday opening. Four men were found drunk in the ty bach, two of them had jugs of beer in their hands, and the defendant's daughter was also found drunk in the house. He was fined £1 + costs and the men were fined 5s each + costs. Unfortunately, old George seemed to have a fondness for attending court. He was fined again for the same offence in September 1877.

By 1891, the landlord was Philemon Collins, and he must have gone to the same publican school as George. He managed to get arrested for permitting drunkenness in April of that year and he was fined 5s + costs. In August, his licence renewal was in doubt due to defective structural arrangements and the conviction for permitting drunkenness, but it was clearly permitted in the end. He was charged again in July 1896 for selling beer on Sunday.

It was not all doom and gloom, though. In June 1897, his daughter "Miss Lizzie Collings [sic] of the Royal Oak Inn, Whitchurch, as a pupil, won the junior pianoforte prize at the Machen Eisteddfod."

In March 1906, Arthur Llewelyn, coal merchant, of the Royal Oak Inn, Whitchurch, was charged at the Llandaff Police Court with stealing 1 ton 2½ cwt of coal. He chose trial by jury and was committed to the assizes, bail allowed. We are left to wonder how he was connected to the pub, but he was later acquitted over a misunderstanding on which pile of coal he was permitted to take his supply from at the coal yard.

The origin of the Royal Oak pub name lies with the story of Charles II allegedly hiding in an oak tree at Boscobel Wood to escape the Roundheads at the Battle of Worcester in 1651. It is difficult to associate this, however, with our pub here. The name seems to have been chosen simply because it is popular and recognisable for a pub, immediately identifying what it would sell to any passer-by.

The Three Elms

The Three Elms is located on what was the old turnpike road out of Cardiff, through to the Taff valley. It was well equipped to be a coaching inn, providing accommodation, stabling and blacksmithing, and uniquely placed on part of

Whitchurch Common occupying the west corner, a gateway to the village beyond it. It is easy to visualise it as being a welcome site for travellers coming away from Cardiff across wild and bleak heathland as they progressed northwards. However, the main building and outbuildings have been remodelled a few times over the years and bear no resemblance to any original structures.

In 1797 the property, including cottages and land, was conveyed in trust to the children of a weaver who died shortly after. It was subsequently conveyed to Edward Lewis, a victualler, and this is likely to be the first sign of it being used to sell ale or beer. On that basis, it is a contender for the oldest pub in our village.

In 1818, Lewis Lewis used the Three Elms in his role as Vice President of the Melin Griffith Friendly Society to arrange meetings, and in 1828, he was tenant of the pub by lease. In 1846, the landlord was George Lewis, which makes you wonder if it was the same George Lewis who was at The Hollybush at this time. By 1848, the landlord was William Lewis, again likely more than coincident with The Hollybush.

The pub was named after three ancient elm trees that were near the Ararat Church, all destroyed in storms, the last one in September 1903, when "An old elm tree – a landmark in Whitchurch Common for nearly 200 years – has also come to grief." It was a popular meeting place for many organisations and hosted many events, a proper hub for the community, and being on the edge of the common, ideally placed to gain from any events taking place there.

One strong thing linking most of these pubs was their involvement with the community. We have read about the various societies that used the pubs for all sorts of social support schemes, and inquiries and inquests were also regular occurrences.

Something you could not escape from back in the day, it seems, was the number of establishments run by or owned by someone called Lewis. At some point, most of our pubs had a Lewis as landlord, people of that name kick-starting The Three Elms and The Hollybush, The Butchers Arms (Whitchurch), whose landlord in 1865 was called George Lewis, and Reuben Lewis with his smithy at The Plough. In 1886, David Lewis was landlord of The Three Horseshoes and William Humphrey Lewis had The Old Ton in 1891. Coincidence, or was running a pub a Lewis thing back in the 19th Century?

If you would like to read more about Whitchurch pubs on the internet, there is a link provided at the end of this book.

The Possible Origin and Meaning of...

There are many parts of Whitchurch where you can't help but wonder how they got their names. Here are just a few to speculate upon:

Merthyr Road. Clearly a reference to the route to Merthyr along what was the old turnpike road, the toll gate being close to the Cross Inn – now the Aneurin Bevan. (Why do people change pub names? They are part of our history and heritage.)

However, it was not always the case. In August 1905, the road from the Common to the Plough was to have been named Hafod Road (not to be confused with High Street).

Heol Don. Sometimes misinterpreted on older maps as Rawl Don, which might have been a corruption of Yr Heol Don, generally understood to be a corruption of Heol Ton – 'ton' being lay land or fallow pasture – this is the road (heol) leading across pasture land to the tithe barn and on to Tongwynlais – lay land of the white stream.

Pendwyallt. The head (top) of two hills (pen dwy allt).

Pantmawr. The large / big hollow.

Pantbach. The small hollow.

Penlline Road. From the 1840 tithe map, we can tell that a stretch of land on the east side of our main road, from the library down to the furniture shop, was owned by John Homfray Esq. He also owned land on the north side of Ty'n y Parc and the woollen factory built there. As Dowlais iron masters, the Homfray family owned Penllyn castle near Cowbridge. Our Penlline Road is likely to be linked.

The batter. Locally, we identify the batter as the embankment upon which Whitchurch Rugby Sports and Social Club (W.R.S.S.C.) is built, which overlooks the Melingriffith estate just below it. There have been many definitions of what a batter might mean, some not too palatable.

One definition is it's an old term used in construction: "Batter, in construction, primarily denotes the intentional slant given to structures like walls, or embankments, to enhance stability and drainage, helping structures resist lateral pressures, whereas, an embankment refers to a constructed mound of earth or stone, often used to raise the level of a road, railway, or to prevent flooding by a river." The word batter is also used to describe the angled or sloping foundation and lower sections of a castle or a castle tower.

College Road. Hwyl Rhiwr Cyrff on 14th-Century maps is interpreted as the lane of the slope of the corpses, the funeral route taken from the parish to the mother church at Llandaff.

More can be found on College Road via the references in the next section.

References

There is a lot more on Whitchurch, should you wish to investigate further. Over recent years, the author has contributed many articles to the People's Collection Wales website. These are freely available and accessible online.

This is what has been published to date:
- Whitchurch 1950s–60s
- Whitchurch Common
- Whitchurch Rugby
- Whitchurch Hockey
- Whitchurch Football
- Whitchurch Pubs
- Whitchurch Ararat Chapel
- Eli Evans
- Island Cottage
- Reuben Lewis
- College Road
- The Philog
- Treoda
- Tongwynlais
- Tongwynlais Rugby
- Tongwynlais – Greenmeadow and Lewis's

- Llandaff Yard
- Llandaff Yard Rugby
- The Cow and Snuffers
- Llandaff Rowing

Ref: The People's Collection Wales website: https://www.peoplescollection.wales

They can all be accessed via the search window on the website. Just type in your interest of choice and press 'Enter'.

Attributions

Every effort has been made by the author to observe copyright restrictions.

Dr William Price graphic:
Public domain. Free for editorial, educational, commercial and/or personal projects. No attribution required.

Newspaper inserts:
The National Library of Wales. The copyright status of the works is unknown. This means that the identity and/or location of a potential rights holder cannot be reasonably ascertained.

Melingriffith Works:
The *Children's Employment Commission 1842* was used, obtained from The Coalmining History Resource Centre website. This states: "The Coal Mining History Resource Centre, Picks Publishing and Ian Winstanley reserve the copyright, but give permission for parts to be reproduced or published in any way provided The Coal Mining History Resource Centre, Picks Publishing and Ian Winstanley are given full recognition."

Other photographs and sketches are the author's own work.

Useful Resources

- The Royal Commission on the Ancient and Historical Monuments of Wales (R.C.A.H.M.W.) *Early Castles*. Ref: https://shop.rcahmw.gov.uk/collections/downloads/products/glamorgan-early-castles-ebook
- *The Book of Llandaff,* National Library of Wales
- British History Online. Ref: https://www.british-history.ac.uk
- Glamorgan History Society. Ref: http://glamorganhistory.org/
- Historic Place Names of Wales https://historicplacenames.rcahmw.gov.uk
- National Library of Scotland (for old maps). Ref: https://maps.nls.uk/os/

These are useful sites, but there are others, ones which you could contribute to and help with history and heritage, not just for Whitchurch, but throughout Wales. Have you ever thought of writing your own material or memoirs, perhaps letting younger generations know about your own life's experience? Perhaps writing a book is too much for you, but there are plenty of ways you could share your story or knowledge about the area you were born and grew up in. Perhaps you would even be willing to share some of your family photos.

You might think of yourself as belonging to the modern generation, but trust me, it won't be long before you will not be. One day, many, many people will value and enjoy your story. Locally, nobody has written about Whitchurch of the 1970s, 80s and 90s, or the early part of the 21st century, what it was like, what happened. What do you remember?

The number of people that say, "I wish I had listened to my mam and dad more" or "I wish I had written that down" is never ending. The place you now know will change, and quickly, so take plenty of photos, even of your own street. AWEN at Whitchurch Library has put in some effort to create an environment where these memories can be saved and shared, and they've done so with very limited resources.

There are some good websites set up to preserve our past on a regional and national level. They are free and user friendly:

- The People's Collection Wales is a government-funded site that encourages involvement. Ref link: https://www.peoplescollection.wales
- The Historic Place Names of Wales. Ref link: https://historicplacenames.rcahmw.gov.uk

Please accept my gratitude for buying this book. The intention has been to share some of the weird and wonderful bits of local information I've uncovered on rainy days for others to enjoy. It is not for profit. If costs are covered or there is enough interest to print another batch, that would be great.

Thanks for reading, even if you borrowed it.

Best wishes,
Terry Chard
Whitchurch,
Cardiff.

(No animals or small children have been harmed and definitely no A.I. has been used in the making of this book.)

As an additional note of gratitude, I would like to mention my publisher and their team for all the hand holding, advice and direction I have been given. It is fair to say that without them, this book would never have got off the ground. Highly recommended if you are ever thinking of the same thing. Effie and Alison J, I salute you.

Author Profile

Terry Chard is a local family man, Whitchurch born and bred at a time of open spaces and farms. He can trace his ancestry back over 200 years living in and around the area. Terry went to Eglwys Wen School, Whitchurch Grammar School and then University College Cardiff, gaining an honours degree in Mechanical Engineering. After pursuing a career in engineering, Terry became a Chartered Engineer and Member of the Institute of Mechanical Engineers in the mid-1980s.

His interest in local history was sparked from living at an early age close to the old Glamorganshire Canal, the Melingriffith Tin Works and the Taff Vale Railway. His father and grandfathers between them worked in or on all of them. He was further inspired by work colleagues with an expert knowledge of the Glamorganshire Canal, and 40 years ago, he helped them to retrace its path from Cardiff Docks to Merthyr.

He has an interest in many sports having played local football for a number of years and he enjoys sketching and watercolour painting. Since retirement in 2011, he has become more active with local history. This started as a rainy-day or winter-time hobby, but Terry acknowledges that it is hard to put down once you start. And, of course, in Wales, there are a lot of rainy days. Over recent years, he has shared some of his research with local groups and given occasional talks to them.

Publisher Information

Rowanvale Books provides publishing services to independent authors, writers and poets all over the globe. We deliver a personal, honest and efficient service that allows authors to see their work published, while remaining in control of the process and retaining their creativity. By making publishing services available to authors in a cost-effective and ethical way, we at Rowanvale Books hope to ensure that the local, national and international community benefits from a steady stream of good quality literature.

For more information about us, our authors or our publications, please get in touch.

www.rowanvalebooks.com
info@rowanvalebooks.com

www.ingramcontent.com/pod-product-compliance
Lightning Source LLC
Chambersburg PA
CBHW040256170426
43192CB00020B/2825